W9-DBW-382

WITHDRAWN

Up Against the Retail Giants:

Targeting Weakness, Gaining an Edge

A. Coskun Samli

THOMSON
™

Australia · Canada · Mexico · Singapore · Spain · United Kingdom · United States

Up Against the Retail Giants: Targeting Weakness, Gaining an Edge
A. Coskun Samli

ISBN: 0-324-23308-6
Printed and bound in the United States of America by Phoenix Book Technology
1 2 3 4 5 6 7 8 9 07 06 05 04

For more information, contact Texere at Thomson Learning, 5191 Natorp Boulevard, Mason, OH 45040. You can also visit our website at www.thomson.com/learning/texere.

This publication is designed to provide accurate and authoritative information in regard to the subject matter covered. It is sold with the understanding that the publisher is not engaged in rendering legal, accounting or other professional services. If legal advice or other expert assistance is required, the services of a competent professional person should be sought.

Composed by: Electro-Publishing

A CIP catalogue record for this book is available from the Library of Congress.

TABLE OF CONTENTS

DEDICATION

This book is dedicated to the hundreds of entrepreneurial retailers with whom I worked who considered generating consumer value the way to profitability. They taught me much. This book is also dedicated to my professor and mentor, Stan Hollander of Michigan State University, who gave me my first start. I am indebted forever.

Preface

This book is for those retailers (or retailers to be) who are entrepreneurial, independent, and creative, but who above all, are capable of critically analyzing and explaining what is happening in the market in terms of their store. Thus, this book addresses those who make a genuine attempt to survive the retail jungle. The book is not a "how-to" book dealing with step-by-step recipes. Rather, it attempts to bring theory and practice together and, by doing so, to give a boost to all, but particularly to small and medium-sized retailers who are entrepreneurial and want to be proactive in creating their own competitive advantage.

Retailing is the moment of truth in the capitalistic market system. If the system is creating consumer value, retailing is the main deliverer of it. Manufacturers' efforts either pay off or are wasted at this level of delivery. In this sense, retailing is the firing line for most marketing plans and managerial decisions as well as for consumer attempts to satisfy their needs and improve their quality of life.

In an earlier book (Samli 1998), I pointed out that retailing, despite its role and importance in the marketplace, has been rather neglected in marketing and management related literatures. Although much sophisticated knowledge has accumulated in the marketing and management field, only a small and rather simplistic portion of this research finds its way to retailing theory and practice. This is despite the fact that about 20 percent of working Americans are employed in the retailing sector. The sector has been neglected either deliberately or by default. The retailing sector employs many business majors who have not even thought of taking a retailing course. This author believes that retailing courses and retailing books that attempt to bring theory and practice together and force decision makers to reason carefully are extremely valuable.

It is critical to see that retail practice is strengthened if the theory behind the practice is understood. This certainly is the goal of this book. A deliberate effort is made here to combine retailing theory and practice. This author firmly believes that understanding the theory behind events provides a proper and successful retailing practice that, in turn, generates more value for consumers and more profit for the retailer.

WILL THERE BE A RETAIL REVOLUTION?

Retailing is bound to take its rightful place in the academic arena. There will be more retailing courses, more retailing research, and clearly more emphasis on generating consumer value through retailing. Not only will retailers hire young people with master's degrees in business, but many of these young people will eventually end up having their own retail establishments as well. Thus there will be more and more small retail establishments owned and operated by well-educated people who have a considerable understanding of retail theory and how such theories can be applied to their own specific businesses. As the society advances economically, consumers seek better values generated by the retailing sector. This powerful stimulus will unleash the retail revolution, which will be primarily carried out by entrepreneurial owner-managers.

This book is aimed at this ambitious and entrepreneurial group of people, who certainly can make a difference in generating consumer value in our society and be rewarded for their efforts in the form of profits. It is also hoped that this book will appeal to professional researchers and consultants because it raises important research-related issues that are pertinent to survival in the retail jungle. As the reader progresses through these pages, it should become clear that this book dwells upon the reasoning generated by cross-germination of theory and practice. The emphasis here, therefore, is on a proactive and strategic orientation based on research, reasoning, theory, and application. Although the primary targets of this book are small and medium-sized retailers, almost all the discussion presented in the book is applicable in large-scale retailing as well.

Exhibit P-1 illustrates the general orientation of this book. Theory, combined with the facts relating to the store in consideration, leads to first planning a strategy, then implementing that strategy, and finally evaluating the performance and activating a control mechanism that can lead to readjustment. Such a model is appropriate for all kinds of retail operations, large and small. The expected retail revolution will certainly have such a sophisticated orientation.

Exhibit P-1. The Key Phases of Retail Marketing Strategy Development

```
┌─────────────────┐                          ┌─────────────────────┐
│   Retailing     │◄────────────────────────►│ Specific Store-Related│
│    Theory       │                          │ Retailing Conditions │
└─────────────────┘                          └─────────────────────┘
         │                                              │
         │            ┌─────────────────┐               │
         ▼            ▼                 ▼               ▼
┌─────────────────┐  ┌─────────────────┐  ┌─────────────────────┐
│  Planning the   │─►│  Implementing   │─►│   Controlling and   │
│   Strategy      │  │  the Strategy   │  │    Readjusting      │
└─────────────────┘  └─────────────────┘  └─────────────────────┘
         │                   │                        │
         ▼                   ▼                        ▼
                    ┌─────────────────┐
                    │   Performance   │
                    │  of the Store   │
                    └─────────────────┘
```

Source: Adapted and revised from Samli, 1998.

GLIDING THROUGH THE BOOK WITH READERS

The book begins with an introduction that identifies the importance and dynamic nature of retailing.

Chapter 1 introduces an important concept that is used throughout this book, differential congruence. It means that as retailers we have to be different enough so that our target market identifies with our unique offerings.

Chapter 2 discusses different layers of retail competition and how each layer impacts our store.

Chapter 3 deals with the major trends in this dynamic sector. Again, if we don't grasp the major trends relating to our business, we may not be able to survive and prosper.

Chapter 4 complements Chapter 3 by discussing the evolutionary process that has been seen in this sector.

Chapter 5 delves into a most important concept, asking "What are the market potentials?" A few approaches are presented here to identify the opportunities that may exist in one identified market.

Chapter 6 takes on the very important task of clarifying how consumers behave and what are the implications of this behavior to the well-being of our store.

Chapter 7 complements Chapter 6 by identifying retail strategy alternatives to be used to satisfy the consumer needs in our market and create consumer value.

Chapter 8 reaches out into the critical area of store image management. In essence, one can argue that retailing is all about developing and maintaining a store image.

Chapter 9 explores the human element of retailing. In smaller-scale retailing particularly, people are the strength of the total operation. How to manage our people, therefore, goes to the heart of how to manage our strength.

Chapter 10 points out that no retail establishment can survive as a well-kept secret. The retailer *must* communicate with its market.

Chapter 11 emphasizes the fact that without a proper merchandise (or service) mix, the retailer cannot function, let alone succeed.

Chapter 12 maintains that pricing is critical in retailing. Without a good price mix, the retailer stands no chance in the retail jungle.

Chapter 13 develops the newly emerging concept of retail logistics. It points out that we must understand when we are part of a larger system and when we are alone in dealing with our target market.

Chapter 14 states that, in the final analysis, retailing is an ongoing process and therefore we can learn and change. Thus we must learn to control and adjust our enterprise.

Throughout this book, reference is made to numerous retailing cases. These reflect more than 35 years of research and consulting. These are all real cases emphasizing the key points of the chapters and illustrating realistically what happens in practice. It is hoped that the reader will be able to relate to these cases and compare them with his or her own experiences. The retail jungle is just that, a jungle, but in a real sense it can also be a wonderful public park where everyone can participate and benefit. It certainly is hoped that this book makes a contribution in that direction.

ACKNOWLEDGEMENTS

No book can be written without the help of many other people, and this one is no exception. Even though as a researcher, teacher, and consultant, I made a point of trying to develop knowledge and wisdom myself, I was totally lucky in associating with many people throughout my long career who helped me immensely. At Michigan State University Stan Hollander not only made a profound impression on me personally, but also gave me an appreciation of the importance of retailing.

I'd like to thank my students at the University of Hawaii, where I taught many summers, who alerted me to international and multicultural aspects of retailing. They did many valuable projects that helped me and helped them in their careers.

Professor Laurence Jacobs of the University of Hawaii interacted with me and collaborated on many projects. We spent many hours exchanging ideas on our favorite topic, retailing. Professor Roger Dickinson of the University of Texas at Arlington always managed to discuss new ideas with me each time I called on him.

Dr. Jay Lindquist of Western Michigan University has always been an inspiration. He and I have done numerous conferences and some important research together. Dr. Robert King has helped me in many ways to develop an academic retailing career.

Professor Adel El-Ansary of the University of North Florida has always been a source of encouragement and important ideas. Professor Joseph Sirgy of Virginia Tech not only has always been there for discussion and interaction, but has also been an important partner in many research undertakings.

My good friend, Ed Mazze, Dean of the College of Business, University of Rhode Island, has discussed many issues related to retailing with me over the years. A young, talented colleague, Robert Frankel, was very helpful in critically analyzing the whole book and making valuable recommendations.

Finally, my student and research assistant, Mehmet N. Ongan of Lerner Stores, was always there to discuss important aspects of retailing. My research assistant, Susann Solle, was very helpful in bringing some of the necessary support materials together.

Our secretaries, Leanna Payne and Carolyn Gavin, must receive much of my gratitude since they were so helpful in deciphering my barely legible handwriting. They also advised me on some editorial points.

I received special encouragement from Michael Czinkota of Georgetown University, the series advisory editor, and from Steve

Momper of Thomson Texere. Without their help this book would not have happened. As with my previous books, Beverly Chapman gave me competent editorial advice. I owe her much gratitude. My dean at the University of North Florida, Coggin College of Business, Earle Traynham, is always encouraging. My department head, Gene Baker, was very patient in listening to my points of view and responding wisely.

Hundreds of my graduate and undergraduate students listened, argued, and agreed or disagreed with me about many points that I make in this book. They were patient, attentive, and genuinely interested in my, at times, somewhat unconventional ideas. I certainly owe them much. Finally, Bea Goldsmith argued with me about many points I raised and quietly and calmly gave her opinions based on her experiences. She made me understand the wonderful world of retailing better.

To the hundreds of retailers with whom I worked, interacted, and exchanged ideas, I certainly hope that I made a contribution to their professional well-being. Many of these retailers also received ideas and information as I did consulting work for them. Again, I certainly hope that we all mutually benefited from these experiences. But I must say, I have learned much from you and I am grateful.

To these and many other people who influenced my thinking and my knowledge base over the years, I extend my heartfelt gratitude. I hope that this book will make a modest but noticeable contribution to the wonderful world of retailing, which would be my repayment to the people who helped me. If many retailers read this book and benefit from it, I will consider myself very fortunate and highly rewarded.

A. Coskun Samli

Introduction

Any viable society must be generating consumer value. That is the fruit of all of the economic and business activity in the society. The consumer value that is generated by that society is delivered through the retailing sector. This makes retailing critical for the well-being of society. However, the retailing sector is also very volatile. Almost constantly, it experiences sharp turbulence.

Dayton Hudson, one of the largest general merchandise retailers in the United States during the early 1980s, had been following a growth strategy based on carrying merchandise that represented quality, fashion, and value. The company had grown from 100 stores to 1,000 stores in fourteen years. This was over 20 percent growth a year. But, during the early 1980s the American economy started changing. Department stores started losing their relative position in the economy. For a while, Americans started frequenting smaller, specialty stores and upscale boutiques. In just about the same period, they started patronizing discount stores for general household needs at low prices.

Dayton Hudson was forced to scale down the growth of their department stores. Sears, the largest retailer in the world for more than fifty years, went through tougher times. It laid off thousands of its employees and closed many stores. In the meantime, Target stores emerged as an upscale, discount department store chain. The number of stores in this chain went up from 216 in 1984 to over 1,100 in 2000.

Domino's Pizza had scaled down its offering from a regular Italian restaurant to just take-out pizza. As a restaurant it did not do well; as a take-out pizza operation, it did very well. In 1984, it had nearly 2,000 units scattered throughout the United States. Their annual sales volume had surpassed $625 million. Since the early 1990s the company experienced a substantial increase in its competition. Domino's sales volume declined in the early 1990s. In 1994, the company decided that it would expand its menu, offering, for example, salads, sandwiches, and chicken wings, along with implementing a new aggressive marketing strategy. The company started growing again.

Publix Supermarkets, an upscale supermarket chain with special emphasis on baked goods and deli departments, had been pursuing a relatively slow but deliberate growth strategy, primarily in better-than-average-income Florida locations. While it operated 351 stores in 1988, that number had gone up to over 700 stores in 2000. The company's sales have been increasing around 10 percent a year. The chain has been emphasizing good service, clean stores, and the pleasure of shopping there.

Again, during that same period Kmart became the number two retailer, but could not change and could not respond to the market dynamics. At the writing of this book, the company is in a state of bankruptcy.

On the other end of the spectrum, Gillies, a small ice cream parlor in a university town in the Southeast, was doing very good business during the summer months, but the long winter months were not profitable enough to stay in business. The manager decided to initiate a change in the offering, particularly for the winter months. The establishment offered a most unusual series of soups and sandwiches, along with interesting mugs, tee shirts, and the like. Gillies has become very successful.

These are only a few examples to illustrate the dynamic nature of the retailing sector and the importance of developing a proper marketing strategy, the kind of strategy that either makes or breaks the individual retailer. These examples also indicate the increasing difficulties of small entrepreneurial retailers trying to survive in the shadow of retailing giants.

Surviving in the shadow of the giants is not easy. It is like trying to survive in a jungle that has many overgrown and not so friendly creatures that could destroy us. However, as we function in that jungle, we learn a lot of things from these giants. Such knowledge could be extremely beneficial for our survival. Perhaps the most alarming feature of the retailing sector can be observed in the small-scale retailing area. Approximately 80–100 thousand small businesses, most of which are retailers, fail and or go bankrupt yearly. Thus, one considers the whole retailing sector a jungle where survival requires a carefully mapped out strategy regardless of whether we are Target or Joanny's Gifts.

In the above examples: Dayton Hudson changed its focus; Domino's expanded its offerings; Publix kept a steady course; and Sears was derailed. But what about those 80,000 or 100,000 retailers that failed? It is quite likely that they did not have a game plan, or their respective strategies simply did not work and they were either so naïve they did not see it soon enough or so inexperienced they couldn't change their course in time.

It is clear that unless the retailer thinks in terms of strategic planning and acts accordingly, the chances of survival followed by growth and prosperity are quite limited. The retail competition is constantly getting keener.

When retail organizations, large or small, make a major shift from the old fashioned orientation of merchandise management—which means only sell, sell, sell—to a strategic marketing orientation of creating customer value, then the probability for success and survival increases. If we want to survive in the retail jungle, a properly implemented strategic marketing plan must be the focal point of our thinking and our functioning. This book is about this vital concept of retailing strategy formulation, development, implementation, and control, particularly for small retailers whose survival in the retail jungle must be based on reality and not a fairy tale.

Every retailer must develop its competitive advantage, which is generated by its strategic posture, its unique way of generating customer value. Every retailer tries to develop a group of satisfied and loyal customers who like to shop at that store, which generates customer value. This means the retailer has competitive advantage. The pursuit of competitive advantage is not a typical orientation. It is not usually found in the average retail marketing situation. It is a skill that needs to be developed. The essence of this book is about developing that skill of creating competitive advantage through strategic planning and implementation. Strategic retail marketing that will improve the chances of survival in the retail jungle requires going beyond day-to-day activities, following simple "how to" approaches, or implementing so-called fail-safe recipes that do not even work.

This author maintains that a series of logical and research-based steps must be performed if a small retail establishment is to stand a chance to become viable and prosperous. Throughout this book, we discuss the conditions that will lead to understanding the sequential steps and tasks that need to be performed so that a successful retail marketing strategy is in place.

First, it is important for the entrepreneurial retailer to realize that one does not need to be "all things to all people." A small boutique, for instance, can do quite well with four or five hundred loyal customers who spend about $2,000 annually for their wardrobe.

RETAIL JUNGLE REVISITED

This section could easily be deemed "Retail Darwinism is alive and kicking." There are a number of very powerful trends that are creating the retail jungle. If we were engaged in the task of starting an independent retail establishment or entering into the retailing arena in one way or another, it is critical that we fully grasp the concept of retail Darwinism. Although partially it means survival of the fittest, in retailing at this point in time it is also *survival of the fattest.*

There are at least four key types of forces that are accelerating retail Darwinism and making this sector truly a jungle for the small and medium-sized retailers. These four types are: market related forces, competition related forces, consumer related forces, and technology related forces. Exhibit I-1 illustrates these factors.

Exhibit I-1. Key Forces Behind retail Darwinism

MARKET RELATED FORCES
• Sluggish growth
• Deflation
• Value chain revolution

COMPETITION RELATED FORCES
• Wal-Mart
• Supercenters
• Warehouse clubs

CONSUMER RELATED FORCES
• More sophisticated and better informed consumers
• Better communication
• Speedier reaction to consumer requirements
• High-quality, low-cost merchandise needs
• More and better service required
• Carefully consumer-focused assortment
• Ethnicity and personalized service

TECHNOLOGY RELATED FORCES
• Smart consumers
• Smart stores
• Scientific retailing

Market Related Forces

The American economy is cyclical. As of the writing of this book the economy is showing signs of recovery from recession. When the economy sneezes, the retailing sector catches pneumonia. Hence many small and vulnerable retailers do not survive.

Similarly during the past few years the American economy experienced something that it had never experienced before, deflation. Prices went down for consumers, but costs for retailers either remained the same or increased. This situation created shrinkage in retail profits. Again those that are vulnerable and functioning on very small profit margins are having a very difficult time.

Retail distribution channels during the past decade or so have been named value chains. As the products throughout the marketing channel approach the retailer, value is added in terms of proximity, form, information, convenience, and the like. As the value chain revolution becomes more and more a reality, large retailers benefited from it because of their size and the sales volumes they generate. This situation created a stronger and stronger relationship between suppliers and large retailers. However, small and medium-sized retail establishments are not quite part of this revolution.

Competition Related Forces

The past three decades or so have seen the trend of the dominance of giant discounters. First Kmart, then Wal-Mart, Costco, Sam's, B.J.'s, and others have emerged. These are categorized as supercenters or warehouse clubs. Their presence has been creating tremendous competition for all types of traditional retailers. Thus, nontraditional retailers have a chance to play a very important role in the American retailing scene.

Consumer Related Forces

Today's consumers are much more informed and sophisticated than their predecessors. As such, they require better communication and speedier reaction from retailers to their requirements, and they expect higher quality merchandise offered at lower prices. They force the retailer to develop carefully customer-focused assortments. And, perhaps above all, they demand more and better services. All of these consumer demands are making the retail jungle a more difficult place in which to function. The last item in this category displayed in Exhibit I-1 may be the key to survival in small-scale retailing, since population estimates indicate that ethnic minorities have a greater rate of population growth than the majority. Thus, ethnicity and commensurate personal service are likely to become more critical than ever before. These are the features small retailers are more capable of delivering.

Technology Related Forces

Information technology not only has enabled and empowered consumers to demand certain products and services as described above, but has also made those who can use new retail technologies smarter in terms of running their operations efficiently and effectively. Thus smart stores are becoming more and more engaged in scientific retailing that is more information based and efficiency oriented. Since mostly large retailers are privy to the most recent and highly sophisticated technologies, they are creating tremendous pressure on small and medium-sized retailers.

OBJECTIVES OF THIS BOOK

Given the hostile atmosphere surrounding the modern retailer, this book offers five important objectives to help every retailer to succeed: (1) to use reason in retail decision-making; (2) to bring theory and practice together; (3) to be able to plan retail strategies; (4) to know how to implement the strategy; (5) to learn how to assess effectiveness (see Exhibit I-2).

Although the book is written with small and medium-sized retailers in mind, these five objectives and the methods to achieve them are equally applicable to larger retail giants as well. It is hoped that the procedures and practices discussed throughout this book would stimulate retail thinking in a proactive manner.

Reasoning Behind Retail Decisions

Above all, this book puts a special emphasis on the fact that behind every retail decision there is a reason. However, in real life not all reasons are based on factual information. Reasoning based on information, experience, and deduction leads in the direction of consistent, long lasting, effective decisions that

Exhibit I-2. The General Orientation to Success

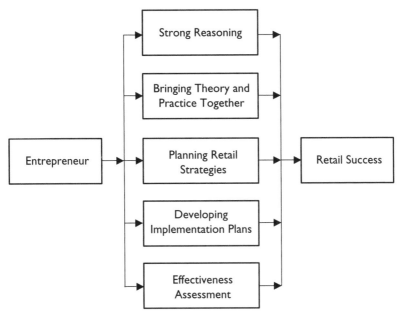

create consumer value as they generate profit. Retailing is not a "catch as catch can" activity, is not a display of whimsical behavior, and, above all, is not another form of gambling. Good retailing is based on understanding the consumers, identifying market forces that play a critical role in our retail establishment, and as a result, reasoning out the best solutions to generate maximum consumer value.

Bringing Theory and Practice Together

The reasoning that is mentioned above must be used in all retailing decisions. Most of the time, this reasoning stems from bringing theory and practice together. A very rich retail research literature (Samli, 1998) can be used in the effort to bring these two together. It is essential to realize that behind every good decision there is a theoretical stance.

Planning the Strategic Posture

All retailers, from the largest to the smallest, must have a game plan. Having a strategic plan implies not only possessing a game plan but also understanding how it is to be implemented proactively. After all, a strategy that cannot be implemented is not likely to become a reality. Unimplementable strategy simply has no value. The modern retailer must be in a position to identify the strategic options and prioritize them. It is in this prioritization stage that implementability becomes an issue.

Implementing the Strategy

Although in choosing the strategy a retailer must consider its implementability, there is a fine line between implementability and the implementation of the strategy. Whereas implementability signifies how a proposed strategy might be put in place to function, implementing the strategy is having concrete plans to make that strategic choice work.

The implementation plan includes five important mixes: (1) goods and services mix; (2) communication mix; (3) pricing mix; (4) human resource mix; and (5) logistics mix. These are discussed in Chapter 1. The content of these mixes and their relative importance are likely to vary from one type of retail store to another, as well as from one geographic location to another. Even the same type of strategic option is bound to have some distinguishing and unique features. Thus, in a sense, every game plan is different and every implementation plan is even more so. This is what makes retailing a fine art, based on some profound logic, reasoning, and facts. This is where the theory and practice meet, which is the essence of improving the probability of success and the opportunity for greater profit. In other words, entrepreneurship that we discuss throughout this book truly comes forth in the implementation of the strategy. Here, being *creative* and being *proactive* are the essential features of success.

Assessing Effectiveness

It is extremely critical to determine if the strategy and its implementation are being successful. If a retailer develops a strategy and a plan to implement it, but does not quite know if these plans are working, that retailer is not likely to survive the retail jungle. The success or lack thereof must be detected very early so if the actual results are deviating from the planned results, then corrective action can take place quickly and effectively. Every retailer must develop its own early indicators that will generate an ability to determine if the business is going in the right direction and is yielding satisfactory results.

Entrepreneurs

Our discussion thus far implies a very strong presence of entrepreneurship in successful retailing activity. Entrepreneurship, by definition, indicates the presence of creativity, leadership, and performance in a totally proactive manner. Entrepreneurial orientation also displays a very strong sense of independence. Although this book inclines in the direction of small and medium-sized retail establishments, it should not be understood that entrepreneurship is related solely to small size. The five-step management activity identified in this book is the general orientation that is used by entrepreneurs towards the success of the retail establishment, regardless of size. Exhibit I-2 illustrates how this orientation leads to success.

The exhibit presents a philosophical picture of this book. Regardless of size, retail decisions must be based on reasoning. Small retailers and large retailers must understand the theoretical underpinnings of their decisions. Entrepreneurial retailers must be able to develop strategic alternatives that will distinguish their stores from others and deliver consumer value. These alternatives must be successfully implemented. The results must always be quickly and accurately assessed.

SUMMARY

Retailing is a very dynamic sector. The dynamic nature of retailing necessitates going with choice rather than chance. Going by choice is applying entrepreneurship in five general areas: using reasoning, bringing theory and practice together, planning retail strategies, developing implementation plans, and assessing effectiveness. This book deals with these five general areas of management activity that are intimately related to entrepreneurship.

REFERENCES

Samli, A. Coskun (1998), *Strategic Marketing for Success in Retailing*, Westport, CT: Quorum Books.

Retail Marketing Strategy Development

A retail establishment must have distinguishing features that will enable consumers to identify it as well as be attracted to it. At the same time, these distinguishing features could dissuade consumers from patronizing the retail establishment. Thus, the unique or distinguishing characteristics of the store must be very appealing to prospective customers. Therefore, we seek congruence between the store's uniqueness and its appeal to its customers.

THE THEORY OF DIFFERENTIAL CONGRUENCE

If the congruence between the store's features and the customers' preferences synergistically becomes the unique features that differentiate the store from others, then the store is optimizing its market opportunities. This means the store, through its offering and its personality, makes a distinct contribution to its customers' well-being. Such synergy improves the store's probabilities of success.

The Legacy of Two Stores

In a small southeastern town there are two upper middle class ladies apparel stores. Store One is located at one end of a busy mall, presenting simple and understated elegance. Store employees (only part-time with very attractive discounts for their own purchases) are well known socialites. The store is run almost as an on-going party. The employees invite their friends to try new merchandise and socialize. The store owner/manager, who is well known in the community, will not allow a customer to leave the store unhappy. There is always a glass of wine, a home-baked cake or exotic tea available for consumption. This little store is

1

extremely profitable because of its *differential congruence*. What it offers and what makes it unique are very well accepted features by its customers. This dynamic synergism is ideal for generating profit and customer value simultaneously.

Store Two is located at the opposite end of the mall. Unlike the first store, it has an overstated elegance. Salespeople are like models from a fashion show. The store looks expensive and formal. Its "special" sales are not quite convincing. The store does have its distinguishing features, but they are not quite appealing to their prospective customers. Store Two has been struggling.

Thus, differential congruence means that the retail establishment has certain distinguishing features that are not only expected but are well accepted. Any successful retail store has certain features that are liked by its customers, which is why they come back and continue patronizing that store. Even the retail stores that are supposed to be quite similar to others, such as fast food places or low-price convenience stores such as the ones that sell tee shirts or casual wear, have certain unique differentiating factors such as location, personnel, or the specials it offers, which can be valued by customers.

In our market system of monopolistic competition, every individual business, because of its uniqueness, is a kind of monopoly. Managing that uniqueness and making it most appealing are the key tenets of a proactive and successful retail management process. This is all about differential congruence. In order to achieve differential congruence, first we must establish retailing goals and, second, we must manage retailing mixes.

ESTABLISHING RETAILING GOALS

If we don't know where we are going, how can we get there? This question is raised a few times throughout this book. The retailer, or the retailer-to-be, must have a critical and achievable goal in mind.

When Sears establishes a goal of good value for the money for the middle class, it does very well. When Wal-Mart aims at the lower middle class with low prices and delivers, it does well. When Bulgari delivers uniquely designed jewelry to the very rich of the world, it does well. When Wendy's aims at mature markets with its hamburgers along with its other fast foods and hit the mark, it does well.

Notice that all of these cases display a very close connection between the goals and the delivery. Just how does a retailer, regardless of size, establish goals? Furthermore, do these goals remain the same in time?

Although there are many alternatives in establishing goals, a few of them must be identified here. Knowing the market quite well perhaps is the key opener to all or, at least, to most other alternatives in establishing goals. If you know the market well, you can think of new opportunities based on what consumers in a given area may need and yet not be receiving. In an area, for example, where income is high and golfing is big, expensive golfing equipment retailing does well. In an adjacent area, however, where income is not so high but aspirations to imitate the expensive lifestyle are high, used golfing equipment and golfing shoe repair may be a very good goal to pursue. Similarly, there may be an obvious gap in the supply and demand of videos or frozen yogurt. When my friend opened a suvlaki place adjacent to a major university, he took advantage of the students who were tired of hamburgers and pizzas but had no other alternatives. He is now a rather rich man. Having special skills that may be useful or needed by consumers is a very good approach. A good short order cook may develop certain dishes that may be very popular, say, with students in a college town. Similarly, working with a franchising company and using its expertise to get a small retail establishment started is a commonly used goal-development activity. Major franchising companies have their own retailing goals that can be localized rather easily and may give a future entrepreneur a good start. But, knowing where to go is far different from getting there. The retailer must use the special features or tools that the retail store has developed. These features are controllable factors that develop and manipulate the retail image and make it suitable to the target market. Thus, the retailer becomes successful as the retail store generates customer value.

MANAGING THE RETAIL MARKETING MIXES

There are five retail-marketing mixes at the retailer's disposal to be used as tools to implement the retail strategies. These are the goods and services mix, the communications mix, the pricing mix, the human resource mix, and the logistics mix as shown in

Exhibit 1-1. Although all of these are discussed later in this book, a brief discussion of each is in order here.

The goods and services mix gives the retailer its reason to exist. The merchandise assortment is by far the key identifying feature of a retail establishment. Payless Shoe Source is known for its limited variety and extremely low prices. Target is known for its reasonable prices and extensive variety of reasonably good quality merchandise. Taco Bell is known for low-priced Mexican food dishes. This list can go on until the last retailer is mentioned. Along with the merchandise, a retail store also offers services. If the merchandise mix is right, services play a synergistic role by complementing it and raising its appeal and the satisfaction it generates.

The communications mix is the way the retailer informs its prospective customers and keeps in touch with its regular customers. No retail establishment can survive and prosper without some promotion. Being a well-kept secret is totally unacceptable. Many small retailers, particularly in small communities, assume that "word of mouth" advertising is more than adequate and that they don't need additional advertising or promotion. This almost invariably backfires. The retailer becomes a well-kept secret. The

Exhibit 1-1. Retailing Mixes

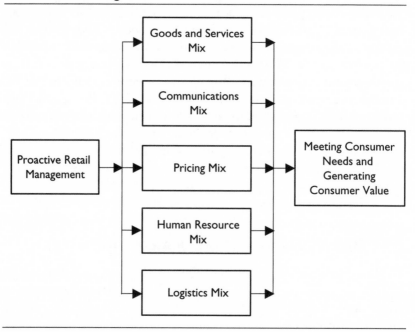

communications mix has a multimedia characteristic, including advertising, personal selling, sales promotion, and the Internet.

The pricing mix has three critical components: efficiency, competition, and image. The first implies the management styles of running the retail establishment. If the establishment is run efficiently, the savings will be passed on to the store's customers through lower prices or increased services. The competitive component indicates that the retail establishment uses price as a major competitive tool. Discount stores, bargain basements, outlet stores, buying clubs, and other similar retail operations use price for that purpose. Many of these emphasize the policy "We will not be undersold, knowingly." Finally, the image component means the store is using its price mix to promote an image of being a reasonable place with some exceptional buys and, overall, good buys. However, such a strategy calls for carefully planned pricing practices without creating price wars with competitors.

The human resource mix, particularly for very small retailers, is a key competitive tool. This is where the basic marketing relationship begins. Specifically, a small retail establishment without a friendly, talkative, knowledgeable, and understanding group of employees who are ready and anxious to serve cannot possibly succeed. The retailing people must have information and empathy for the consumer and must be able to pass that along to their customers. This is true for both the selling and nonselling personnel of the retail establishment. If the human resources of the retail establishment go out of their way to help customers in every way necessary, those customers will come back again and again. Furthermore, they will bring others along with them.

The logistics mix has two key and distinct components: in-store logistics and out-of-store logistics. In-store logistics, providing proper merchandise combinations in the right places, moving the merchandise swiftly from storage to where it is displayed for sale, and making sure that on-shelf performance is high are just some of the extremely critical activities for retail success. Out-of-store logistics means having a quick response system on the part of the retailer, activating the merchandise mix replenishment by suppliers in the most cost-and time-efficient manner. These two aspects of logistics must be kept in balance for optimal results.

SYNERGISM AMONG THE MIXES

Retailing, in essence, is constructing an image and managing it by re-enforcing, by strengthening, or by changing. All of the five mixes have a store image component. All of the activities related to the five mixes have a direct or indirect impact on the overall store image management. Whether the image is being developed, maintained, or modified, all of the components of all five mixes must work together. Otherwise, they may nullify each other, and the store may perform submarginally. Consider, for instance, Food Lion. As a large grocery store chain, it was trying to establish itself as the lowest cost and most value providing outlet, but many of its prices were, in fact, higher, and in a few occasions, the products in its warehouses were not in the best possible shape in terms of freshness and sanitation. These mistakes were corrected swiftly, but suboptimal performance as a result of the negative image has continued. It must be understood that the market has a memory, so it does not forget, and it does not forgive easily. Lack of congruence among the retail mix components can create suboptimal performance. But if the retail mixes are all working well and the retail establishment is aiming at the wrong target market, that means it is lacking *differential congruence*, which is deadly.

IMAGE MANAGEMENT IS THE KEY

As can be seen, managing the store image can be equated with the overall retail marketing management. Customers going to Cartier's, Neiman Marcus or Wal-Mart know what to expect, and they therefore make a deliberate choice. It is this choice that is expected to take place when the store image is managed properly; that is, the store is projecting an image which is confirmed by its strategic retail mix management.

The store image is obviously critical. It represents all the aspects of communication that the store performs through its retail mixes in a market and towards a market segment or a niche market. It must be reiterated that the store image is synergistic. It has numerous components such as store appearance, sales people's attitudes, merchandise mix, internal layout, and many others. But the store image, as a result of synergism, is more than the sum total of all of these elements.

Regardless of whether the image is existing or aspired to, it is the key in formulating and implementing strategy. If the store is aiming at the older and well-to-do segment, a dynamic youthful image is not likely to do the job. To illustrate: the Glo-Wood Restaurant was located adjacent to a major metropolitan university. It was kept open twenty-four hours a day, seven days a week. It catered primarily to students and unskilled blue-collar workers residing in that particular area. A good atmosphere of communication and relaxation prevailed in the restaurant. Food was cheap, and waitresses were friendly. The restaurant was always very crowded and was very successful. When the owners retired, they sold it. The new owner wanted to make the restaurant an elegant, high-class place. He changed the interior, the menu, and the appearance of the establishment. In less than six months, he was out of business. The elegant image he tried to create was not acceptable to the existing market segment. The regular customers did not feel comfortable in the new setting that he created (Samli, 1998).

It is not possible to develop a marketing strategy without paying attention to the existing image and the market in which the current operations are taking place. Here it is critical to identify two types of images: intended and perceived. For a successful retail establishment, these two must be the same. Consider the following: a bank in the Midwest considered itself to be the elite or upscale bank in the community, catering to the upper-middle and upper socio-economic classes. It had been promoting an image accordingly. The services it offered were more expensive and comprehensive. The services it offered were more unique than typical banks. Its interior layout was rather plush. However, research undertaken by the nearby university indicated that the bank actually was catering to the lower-middle class. Its customers did not care for all the frills that the bank offered. The discrepancy between the intended and actual image is rather clear. The bank was wasting a lot of money and effort trying to project an image that was not acceptable. If the intended and actual images are not the same, the expected customer satisfaction–driven customer loyalty cannot be achieved. Exhibit 1-2 illustrates three relationships between the intended and actual store images. It reiterates that the intended and actual images must be one and the same for the firm to optimize its performance.

However, even if the intended and actual images are the same, how the retailer arrived at this point is critical. From this

Exhibit 1-2. The Workings of Differential Congruence

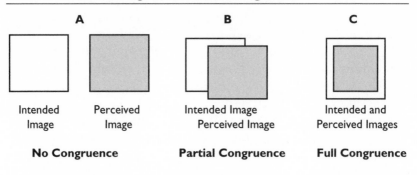

A	B	C
Intended Image Perceived Image	Intended Image Perceived Image	Intended and Perceived Images
No Congruence	**Partial Congruence**	**Full Congruence**

Source: Adapted and revised from Samli, 1998.

Note: Full congruence implies that the management of the store and the store's consumers are all in sync.

perspective, the retailer can develop proactively, reactively, or inactively.

Developing the right kind of image proactively implies that the retailer makes a clear-cut decision about its goals, goes after these specified goals, and succeeds. Such a strategic orientation always leads to success. Being the best jeweler or the best Chinese restaurant in a given market area are examples of such goals and accomplishments.

Developing the right kind of image reactively implies that although the retailer wanted to be the best jeweler in the specified market, it is not being perceived as such. It is perceived perhaps as the place that is quite reasonable and sells good value. The retailer needs to change and adjust the retail mix strategies accordingly. If this adjustment is not made, much will be lost in terms of claiming certain things and not succeeding. This, in time, can be very harmful since the retailer is not displaying consistency in its strategic functioning.

Although it is almost pure luck, the retailer may not have a specific goal and a plan of action, but such inactive behavior pays off. The retailer is perceived by the market as not having any key claims, but is doing a good job for the walk-in customers regularly. Again, if this is the picture, the retailer must adjust the strategy accordingly.

It is obvious that proactive image building provides much greater market power and resultant profit. Many retailers fall into the third category of inactive image building; few of them succeed and many fail.

SUMMARY

Retail marketing strategy is critical for survival. Every retailer must have a game plan to fulfill its goals and generate customer value, which is the essence of profitability. This game plan is the retail strategy. In order to develop a proper retail marketing strategy, the retailer must appreciate the theory of differential congruence. In other words, the retailer must know that its unique features are what its customers expect, and such congruence distinguishes that retail establishment from others.

In order to develop differential congruence, the retail establishment must have some specific goals regarding its target audiences and a strategy to achieve them. The retailer uses five groups of strategic tools to develop a strategy. These groups of tools are called retail mixes. There are five retail mixes: goods and services, communications, pricing, human resources, and logistics. If all of these mixes work together, the retailer will optimize the overall performance by creating customer value and maximizing profits.

REFERENCES

Samli, A. Coskun (1998), *Strategic Marketing for Success in Retailing*, Westport, CT: Quorum Books.

2

Fitting Into Multi-Layered Retail Competition

Saks Fifth Avenue competes with Neiman Marcus rather directly, but in a very indirect manner it may be competing with Dollar Stores that are the resurrection of old five and dime stores. Because of the accessibility of the retailing facilities and variety of their offerings and because of the mobility of consumers and the desire on the part of many to get a better buy, all retailers are competing with each other.

In order to survive and succeed in the retailing sector, it is important to understand the nature and intensity of retail competition. In the retail jungle there are five distinct layers of retail competition. Any retailer and any retailer-to-be must be very familiar with all of these layers and must understand how each impacts the particular establishment in question. Placing oneself in the right layer implies understanding the nature of the competition a retailer must be equipped to face.

Exhibit 2-1 illustrates the layers of retail competition from the most basic nuts and bolts type of competition to the broadest market competition. Each layer indicates a different type of retail competition that one needs to understand if one wants to survive the retail jungle. As can be seen, our discussion deals with five layers.

LEVEL ONE

This is the most common type of competition. Every retailer must offer a combination of its five retail mixes. This is how it survives and succeeds. But all retailers cannot offer such a positive combination. Those that can put together the best combination for their intended markets are those who are likely to succeed. Here the *turnover classification theory* comes into play. Those products that have high turnover rates are typically convenience products

Exhibit 2-1. Levels of Retail Competition

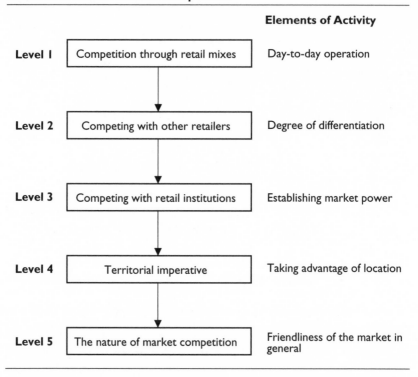

		Elements of Activity
Level 1	Competition through retail mixes	Day-to-day operation
Level 2	Competing with other retailers	Degree of differentiation
Level 3	Competing with retail institutions	Establishing market power
Level 4	Territorial imperative	Taking advantage of location
Level 5	The nature of market competition	Friendliness of the market in general

that are consumed or purchased very often and have low mark-up levels. Exhibit 2-2 illustrates four scenarios. The upper left quadrant of the exhibit shows a rather unlikely situation—high turnover and high mark-up. Products that have high turnover typically have low mark-up. However, this is an exceptional situation, where for a short period of time some special products may be very much in demand. Certain fashion goods may be in that group, but only temporarily.

The lower left quadrant indicates the normal case of high mark-up and low turnover. Typically, luxury items and some consumer durables, such as appliances, cars, and computers, fit in that category.

The upper right hand corner also indicates the standard condition. Products with low mark-up typically have high turnover rates. Most convenience products are in that category. 7-Eleven stores thrive on such merchandise mix characteristics.

Finally, the lower right quadrant displays the most difficult scenario. If a retailer's products are mostly low mark-up and low turnover, and they remain that way for a long while, then that

Exhibit 2-2. Margin Turnover Classification Theory

		MARK-UP LEVELS	
		HIGH ← → LOW	
		Special short-lasting products fashion goods, limited-supply products	**Convenience products** consumer nondurables, groceries
TURNOVER RATE	HIGH LOW	**Luxury items** expensive products, jewelry, expensive cars	**Introductory products** some shopping goods, some pharmaceuticals

retailer is in a difficult position. It has too many introductory products that are not gaining momentum in the marketplace, or it has shopping goods that are not selling well and thus it must offer large discounts.

Although department stores or discount stores carry products that fall into each of the four categories illustrated in Exhibit 2-2, there is also a natural tendency for products to group. Hirschman coined this *natural dominance theory*, which states that certain product groups made available through certain retail establishments have the tendency to become high class and attract a variety of products. For example, Bloomingdale's carries products and brands that consumers know are borderline luxuries. One might ask to what extent underwear or neckties could be luxurious. They could be perceived as luxury products if they are purchased, say, in Bloomingdale's or at Neimann-Marcus. If they are likely to be perceived as special or luxury products, they generate more consumer value based on the reputation of the retailer. But the critical aspect of natural dominance theory is that next to a Bloomingdale's there will not be Payless Shoe Source or a Chinese take-out restaurant. Indeed instead, there will be a Cartier's or Saks Fifth Avenue, indicating that there is a priority ordering in grouping of retail establishments. Exhibit 2-3 illustrates some details of the natural dominance theory.

Moreover, according to natural dominance theory, there is also a priority ordering in the groupings of these retail establishments. Again, next to a Neimann Marcus there will be a Saks Fifth Avenue, and similarly, there will be expensive jewelry, decorative home accessories, and classical upscale apparel.

Exhibit 2-3. Natural Dominance in Retailing

HIGHEST QUALITY

Cartier's

Saks Fifth Avenue

Bloomingdale's

Charles Jordan

Tiffany's

Lerner's

Victoria's Secret · Sears · Limited Express · **HIGHEST PRICES**

Soft Goods Staples

Waldenbooks Major Appliances

Dollar Tree

Home Depot

Wal-Mart

Eckerd Drugs

Payless Shoes

Small Electronics

Home Improvement

Health and Beauty Aids

Source: Adapted and revised from Samli, 1998.

In a middle class setting, there may be a Sears, surrounded by Victoria's Secret, Limited Express, and the like. In terms of product categories, staples, soft goods, books, appliances and consumer electronics are all likely to be brought together.

By the same token, in a low to lower-middle class setting, one would find a Wal-Mart surrounded by Eckerd Drugs, Payless Shoe Source, and Home Depot, among others. Product groupings will be small electronics, home improvement, health and beauty aids, and groceries.

Natural dominance theory basically would apply to all five of the five retail competition levels. It is essential to realize that a Dollar Tree Store would not do well if it were located next to, say, Bloomingdale's. Between the turnover classification and natural dominance theories, many retailing successes and failures can, at least partially, be explained. However, there is more to be said about the four levels that have not been discussed so far.

LEVEL TWO

Exhibit 2-1 describes this level as "competing with other retailers." At any given time, in population centers such as cities or towns, many retail establishments that are similar to each other are competing. Sears, Wal-Mart and Kmart, Kroger and Winn-Dixie are among these.

All of these stores are involved in attempting to develop competitive advantage and compete with each other. Samli (1998 and 1989) has identified four generic forms of competition at this level. These are all intra-institutional ways of developing competitive advantage that translate to differential congruence. These four generic forms are imitation, deviation, complementation, and innovation (Samli 1998). The following is a brief description of these four generic competitive practices.

Imitation

As seen in Exhibit 2-3, all retailers have certain traditional lines of merchandise that everyone knows they carry. Carrying certain basic inventories, therefore, is logical and necessary. A basic inventory that will appeal to the "core" market is a must. From that perspective, if one were to analyze the depth and breadth of inventories carried by Wal-Mart and Kmart or the menus offered by McDonald's and Burger King, one may not find any significant difference. The core markets here are similar, especially for larger retailers. Hence, it is natural that their merchandise or service mixes overlap.

Many small retailers also use imitation as a method of competition. In such cases, small retailers that do not have a clear-cut mission or a well-defined target market may imitate the large retailer to stay in business by taking away a small part of its business. For example, a shirt and tie specialist that is located next to Sears follows that kind of imitation competition. The specialist will have a narrower but deeper inventory and would expect to pick up part of the Sears traffic.

Deviation

Despite the fact that many retailers imitate each other at their core activity, they also deviate from each other in practice. This deviation differentiates the retailer and identifies it in terms of its uniqueness. Deviation, just as imitation, is also exercised by the use of retail mixes. All of these mixes contribute to the retailer's overall image. Thus, even though Wal-Mart and Kmart overlap in 80 percent of their activities, media mixes, product-service, price, human resource, and logistics mixes, at least 20 percent of difference distinguishes the two. In fact, this 20 percent is extremely critical for managing a particular clientele. Although grocery chains such as Publix, Harris Teeter, or Winn-Dixie may be overlapping about 85 percent, one may have more produce, the other may put more emphasis on gourmet lines, and yet another may have some concentration on ethnic products. Again, that 15 percent can be very critical in establishing competitive advantage.

Complementation

Many consumer products are sold most readily when the choice that is offered is greater and when that choice is supported with other products and services complementing it. This particular principle is critical in retailing shopping goods. When consumers are shopping around for better quality and price, in short, better bargains, they will be more satisfied if they have greater options to choose from. This is why the stores mentioned earlier, in discussing natural superiority theory, gather together to compete with each other as well as to complement each other. The tie rack mentioned earlier that is located next to Sears is complementation. It offers a better selection to Sears customers. An ice cream parlor that is selling somewhat exotic flavors and a large variety of ice creams near to a gourmet restaurant may do well since after a big meal many customers of the restaurant may not wish to eat a heavy dessert but may desire a refreshing finish. This is complementation.

Innovation

In the final analysis, retail establishments compete with all comers through their innovativeness by generating a differential advantage. The retail establishment, by carrying unique merchandise, by handling the merchandise differently, by serving its customers in more unconventional ways, or even by having personnel that behave differently, can manage its name and image more uniquely than its competitors. A few years ago, Pizza Hut's eating the pizza the wrong way campaign and McDonalds' giving away beanie babies when these were very popular were examples of innovative behavior. Although innovative competition carries more risk and higher cost factors, there is also a greater opportunity to establish or enhance the store's competitive advantage. Similarly, understanding and utilizing technological advances can also be part of this innovative process.

Of these four, small retailers may be more inclined to go into imitation and complementation, since these are easier and less costly avenues. However, more entrepreneurial and creative retailers may opt for innovation. Although relatively more risky than others, this option is likely to be more profitable. Understanding these four generic competitive practices and choosing one deliberately is likely to put the retailer into a more competitive stance.

LEVEL THREE

The third level, as presented in Exhibit 2-1, is competing with retail institutions. Inter-institutional retailing is rather common in our market economy. Different types of retail establishments have emerged on the American scene during the past thirty-five years or so. Many of them manage to survive and coexist.

Exhibit 2-4 lists many of these retail establishments and identifies their strategic powers. This is how inter-institutional competition in retailing works. As can be seen in the exhibit, some of these retail institutions have only one advantage, price. Box stores and warehouse stores exclusively emphasize price. But specialty stores, such as The Limited or Gap, have more pluses. This is why they are so resilient and, despite increasingly unfriendly conditions in the marketplace, they manage to survive. Supercenters, which are conveniently located, low-price, high-variety retail facilities that concentrate on one-stop shopping, may become more of a threat than others. They seem to be attracting customers from distances as far as 100 miles away(Leah 1995, Flikinger 1995, Samli 1998). If small retailers were to be considered, perhaps all the mixes—location, price, product mix, service, personnel, promotion, and logistics—need to be favorable to survive. This, of course, makes small retailing management very challenging. All of these mixes must be carefully planned and used if one wants to survive the retail jungle.

Exhibit 2-4. Retail Mixes as Strategic Tools*

TYPE OF RETAILER	LOCATION¹	PRODUCT MIX	SERVICE	PERSONNEL	PROMOTION	PRICES	LOGISTICS
Convenience Stores (7-11, Gate, etc.)	+	−	−	−	−	−	−
Supermarket (Kroger, Publix, etc.)	+	+	+	+	+	+	+
Combination Stores (Kmart, Wal-Mart, etc.)	−	+	−	+	+	+	+
Superstore (Albertson's)	−	+	−	+	+	+	+
Box (Limited Line) Store (Jewel T)	+	−	−	−	+	+	+
Warehouse Store (Sam's, Costco, etc.)	−	−	−	−	+	+	+
Specialty Stores (The Limited, Gap, etc.)	+	+	+	+	+	+	−
Supercenter (Safeway, Fred Meyer)	+	+	−	−	+	+	+
E-Tailers	+	+	−	−	+	+	−

(+ = advantage, - = neutral or disadvantage)

*Although typically goods and service mix is the general management tool, in this diagram the two were separated for special impact.

¹Although location is not a retail mix, once it is decided upon it becomes a given. However, in comparing different retail institutions, location plays a significant role as a competitive tool.

Source: Adapted and revised from Samli, 1998.

LEVEL FOUR

This level deals with the geographic superiority or territorial imperative of the retailer. The place where the retailer is located can easily be construed as the most important factor in retail survival. This spatial dimension of retailing has three key dimensions: location of the town where the store is, location of the shopping complex in which the retail store is sited, and the actual location of the store itself.

The Town

Location of town typically relates to out-shopping. People who live in Small Town A may go many miles to shop at Larger Town B because of selection, prices, and even perhaps the pleasure of shopping. Clearly, the town in which the retail establishment is located is a significant consideration. Some cities or towns are more dynamic and provide a better overall market potential for the retail store. On the one hand, the town or even the city may be a sleepy one. Some people there may be quite satisfied with the status quo, but others may be quite unhappy with the retailing facilities that exist in the town. The overall sets of alternatives, the services, the prices, proximities and parking, among other considerations, could be quite unacceptable. It is critical for the retailer to understand the difference between these two opposing orientations.

The Shopping Complex

The concept of territorial imperative comes more into focus when there are identifiable patronage preferences exhibited or expressed toward a given shopping complex in which the retail store may consider locating or is already located. This particular complex could be a major shopping center, a cluster, string street, string mall, a regional mall, or downtown, among others. Each one of these choices would have its own strengths and weaknesses that our retail establishment must consider carefully before locating there. These strengths and weaknesses must be re-evaluated periodically because, in time, such features change.

If consumers, for a series of special reasons, prefer to go to a particular shopping complex and become loyal to it, this loyalty spills over to all of the stores in this complex. The retail establishments in the complex present a synergistic front. If our retail establishment can locate in a complex of this type and manage to fit in, it will certainly benefit from this synergistic front that attracts many customers.

It is critical to realize that a retailer, at any given time, has multiple location options and hence must realize that location is a retail variable tool. This variable tool is particularly important before retail operations commence. Once the retail establishment becomes an ongoing operation, it is too late to take advantage of multiple site options. When it is obvious that the existing location is no longer functional, then the retailer may have to quickly choose a better site.

Specific Site of Our Store

In addition to the town itself and the location of the shopping complex, the specific site chosen for our store is obviously very critical. Consider, for instance, a neighborhood fast-food store or an ice cream parlor. These and other similar types of stores may not have any other distinguishing features and by themselves do not bring customers in. Because of a very favorable location selection, they may establish a competitive advantage. If they can fulfill their target market needs, these stores can generate substantial profits. They develop their own competitive advantage and generate profit as they create consumer value. As can be seen, the spatial dimension of retailing could easily yield competitive advantage leading to differential congruence.

Ability to choose good locations becomes even more critical for multi-unit retail chains. Major retailers such as Target, Wal-Mart, International House of Pancakes, or Holiday Inn all must have specific location criteria that will generate optimal results. Imagine what happens if Charles Jordan ends up locating next to a barber shop or Bulgari Jewelers locates next to a Dollar Tree store that sells odds and ends all priced at one dollar. All of the units in such chains must show consistency in terms of proximity to other stores and in terms of the economic and social features of their respective location. Again, it is rather obvious that small retailers do not have the luxury of using a free-standing location. By definition, small and medium-sized retailers must locate in attractive locations because they cannot draw large groups of consumers. But they can accommodate large groups if these groups are already there.

LEVEL FIVE

Level five describes the prevailing retail competition in the broadest possible manner. The retailing sector, in essence, is a good example of monopolistic competition. Here all establishments are unique in their own way, with no two exactly alike because of their merchandise mix, promotion mix, price mix, human resource mix, logistics mix, location, layout, and other unique features. Each and every retail establishment has a certain degree of monopoly power. Because of this power, its demand curves are shifted to the right and become relatively inelastic. If the demand curve is shifted to the right, it means there will be more units of products sold at any price. And, when the demand curve becomes more inelastic, it means that the retail establishment is gaining economic power displayed in terms of loyalty. Within reason, the increased economic power means loyal customers will pay more for the products rather than switch to another store. However, these conditions depend on the type of store and the type of merchandise. The customers of Gucci or Bulgari are more likely to be loyal to these stores than the customers of Kmart or 7-11. Though this power should not be abused, Gucci can raise its prices and can get away with it. On the other hand, it will be rather difficult, if not impossible, for Kmart to raise its prices because it has much less monopoly power.

Samli (1998) posits that less than perfect competition is the realistic way of describing the milieu of retailing. Hence, each retailer faces somewhat different demand elasticity generated by the competitive advantage specific features of that store have managed to form, leading to differential congruence. Thus, the monopolistic competition setting within which the American retailing sector functions provides the opportunity for all retailers to employ competitive managerial skills and imagination.

A retailer, any retailer, must understand the conditions of monopolistic competition that are discussed in any standard economics textbook. This is a must because these retailers function, survive, prosper, or fail under these conditions.

The conditions of monopolistic competition are (1) relative ease of entry, (2) relative ease of exit, (3) less than perfectly elastic demand, (4) less than perfect information for the individual retailer, (5) the possibility of acquiring additional information, and (6) less than rational consumers with varying degrees of information (Samli 1998). The retailer has to know these conditions and be able to establish differential congruence accordingly.

Although lack of information or the prevailing lack of rationality can tempt the retailer to advertise and promote more to convince the consumers about, say, the best buys at best prices that are available there, such claims should not be outrageously out of line. Otherwise the whole activity can be useless or even self-destructive. If the claims of the retailer are not believable, then those claims create a credibility gap and make conditions worse for the retail store. Thus, the skills to achieve competitive advantage, or to know how far one can go and where one must stop, are not simply skills that all retailers are born with. In fact, those skills require know-how, information, and experience. While some retailers have these skills instinctively and some others can acquire them rather quickly, many other retailers may never possess them. Successful retailing strategy is necessary to meet with and excel in retail competition at all of the five levels that are presented in this chapter.

SUMMARY

Retail competition is very keen, and it happens at five distinct levels. This chapter discusses all of these briefly. Starting with the very specific and going to the broadest levels of retail competition, an attempt is made to describe them. These five levels are competition through retail mixes, competing with other retailers, competing with retail institutions, the territorial imperative of retailers, and the nature of market competition.

The chapter presents two important retail competition theories. The first is margin versus turnover classification, and the second is natural dominance theory. Both are rather important in judging the chances of survival of a retail establishment.

The chapter treats retail location decisions under the title of territorial imperative. The importance of, and options in, retail location decisions are considered.

Finally, a critical discussion is presented regarding the nature of market competition. It must be reiterated that the retailer must be cognizant of all of these levels of competition and how a retail establishment should behave in each. This is not saying that all the competition is within each level. On the contrary, there is always significant competition between the levels as well. It is up to the individual retailer to decide which aspect of competition is more critical for survival and success.

REFERENCES

Flikinger, Burt P. III (1995), "Wal-Mart vs. the World: Who Wins?" *Progressive Grocer*, April, 19.

Hirschman, Elizabeth C. (1979), "Retail Competitive Structure: Present and Potential," in *Educators Conference Proceedings*, ed. Neil Beckwith et al., Chicago: American Marketing Association.

Leah, Rikard (1995), "Supercenters Entice Shoppers," *Advertising Age*, March, 1-10.

Samli, A. Coskun (1989), *Retail Marketing Strategies*, Westport, CT: Quorum Books.

Samli, A. Coskun (1998), *Strategic Marketing for Success in Retailing*.

3

Major Trends in the Retailing Sector

A retailer must be aware of national as well as local trends. The smaller the retail establishment, however, the less important are national trends. It is quite likely that national trends may not carry out to small localities. However, they do generate a trickle effect. Retail establishments, particularly small retailers, must be more aware of local conditions such as a major change in the local highway system that would redirect local vehicular traffic and change the traffic on which local retailers rely. Similarly, the announcement of a major discount retailer locating outside of town or the change in the town's development plans, say, from east side to west side, may be more critical to local small retailers than the stock market crash or a recession in the national economy. This does not mean that local small retailers should not know or, worse yet, not understand national trends. It simply means that retailers must be more aware of local conditions that may have an immediate impact on their well-being.

WHAT IS IMPORTANT IN RETAILING NATIONALLY

Perhaps the most important national retailing trend is in direct marketing. Direct marketing is a type of retailing in which consumers are exposed to goods and services through a nonpersonal medium. They can order and purchase products and services by mail, telephone (Samli 1998), and more recently and more importantly by e-trading. For a while cable TV played a critical role, but more recently purchasing through the Internet via e-trading has surpassed cable TV as a retail medium.

The second major national trade is the resurgence of wholesale discount places (or warehouse stores) such as Costco, Sam's and BJ's. These establishments provide a tremendous variety at low prices. They do not present a very attractive retail ambience;

however, they are very popular. They are expanding and are likely to continue to do so.

The third major trend is in discounting. Discount department stores such as Wal-Mart and Target are performing much better than traditional department stores. Perhaps it is critical to note that in recent years Wal-Mart has expanded its operations into grocery retailing as well. This move not only radically reformulates the grocery retailing sector, but also reiterates the power of discounting.

After a period of about ten years of decrease in the number of retail stores per 1,000 of population, this number has started to increase again. This is the fourth major trend.

Finally, old, reputable, high-class retail establishments have remained in business comfortably and still capture a reasonable portion of the market.

Retailers must follow and learn to interpret these trends. They may modify their practices to adjust to them and improve their probability of survival. Exhibit 3-1 illustrates all six important retailing trends and gives some reasoning behind each.

Exhibit 3-1. Consumer-Driven Key Retailing Trends

TRENDS	CASUAL FACTORS
E-tailing.	More elderly than ever before, more computer ownership, more busy consumers who don't have time to shop.
Wholesale discount places are multiplying.	The relative income of the lower-middle class has been stagnant, hence they need good values.
Discount department stores are emerging.	Consumers' need for lower price and large varieties with more convenience than what wholesale discounters offer.
Retail stores per 1,000 of population are increasing.	The need for convenience as a countertrend of the need for low prices. Consumers want convenience products to be located nearby.
High-class retailing is maintaining its existence.	The relative importance of the upper class has increased more than proportionately. They maintain their loyalty to high-class retailing facilities.
Franchising has continued to grow sharply.	The need to be entrepreneurial and independent, while reducing risk by using already tried and successful retailing practices.

E-tailing, or "clicks as it is referred to in retailing practice, has increased because of convenience for those who are not very mobile and for busy consumers and certainly for computer owners. By the mid-1990s there were, however, ill-fated retailers who thought they could continue retailing without having "bricks and mortar." They closed down their shops to minimize cost and soon realized that they had made a huge mistake, with most of them failing. But to a limited extent in some lines of retailing, as a supplement to regular retailing, e-tailing has continued. Particularly, when regular brick and mortar retailers added e-tailing capabilities they have done rather well.

During the 1990s, American income distribution developed an unconventional pattern. While middle class incomes were stagnant, lower class incomes started shrinking. At the same time, upper class incomes increased substantially. As a result of these developments, the next four trends presented in Exhibit 3-1 emerged. Both discount wholesale and discount department stores have appealed to the middle class with stagnant incomes and to the lower class with decreasing income. But as incomes appear to be somewhat discouraging, it appears that consumers have more refined values and greater variety of needs. Thus, discount wholesaling and discount department stores seem to be enjoying increasing degrees of popularity.

At the same time, either because consumers are working long, hard hours or because they are becoming more convenience prone, there seems to be an increase in the number of retail stores per 1,000 of population. Particularly, there has been an increase in convenience stores, small local fast food eating places, and other necessary services such as video stores or dry cleaning services.

The next trend in Exhibit 3-1 relates to the resilience of high-class retailing. With the substantial increase in income of the upper income group in our society, high-class retailing has been getting a shot in the arm. Some of the very expensive upscale retailers are doing well, and their future appears positive. Currently there are experiments with the possible development of upscale retailing malls. It is not clear if such a thing will truly materialize and be successful; however, it is clear that upscale retailing is likely to expand if income distribution in American society continues its current patterns.

The final trend in Exhibit 3-1 deals with franchising. Franchising involves a contractual arrangement whereby the franchisee is allowed to buy out a part of a large multi-unit chain.

Here individual ownership is enhanced and risk is reduced because of the help franchisors render to franchisees. Individual ownership in this case, however, does not mean a full-fledged entrepreneurship since franchisors specify the characteristics of the business by prototyped stores, standardized product lines, and cooperative advertising. During the past two and a half decades, franchising sales in American retailing have more than tripled (Berman and Evans 2002). Franchising also has been a powerful driver of the global expansion of retailing. From fast food establishments to discount department stores, many international franchising arrangements have emerged. It is critical to realize that most franchising arrangements provide some degree of freedom for individual units such as adjusting their product mixes and localizing their appeals and services. To this extent, some 600,000 franchisees of different types throughout the United States can benefit from many ideas that are presented throughout this book. The emergence of the Internet as a competing retailing alternative has also created a side trend in that many existing retailers who wanted to offer something special to their customers started thinking of some entertainment for them so that they will find it fun to shop. In addition to consumer-driven trends, there are also organizational trends in retailing.

ORGANIZATIONAL TRENDS

The dynamic nature of the markets with which the retailing sector interacts forces retailing organizations to make changes as well. Up until 1992, the number of incorporated retail establishments increased. The number of corporations as a percent of total retail population was the highest in 1987. Since then, this percentage has gone down from 42.7 percent to 30.0 percent of the total of all retail stores. This reinforces the fourth trend reported in Exhibit 3-1, in that there have been many small independent, nonincorporated retailers that have emerged during the past decade or so. But the decline in the number of corporations as a percent of total retail establishments may also imply the many mergers and buy-outs in this area. The fact that the sales volume share of retailing corporations is at an all time high, with a percentage share of over 90 percent of total retail sales, indicates that there is a concentration of power. When the number of institutions gets smaller while their share of total sales gets bigger, it implies that there is much merger and acquisition activity.

Thus, it can be maintained that two developments are coinciding simultaneously. First, merger and acquisition activity is growing, which is creating a concentration of economic power. Second, small but well-established upscale retailers are also doing well.

Furthermore, understandably, many of these incorporated retailers are also chains. Almost 16 percent of all retailing establishments are a part of a chain. This proportion has gone down from about 22 percent in 1982. However, the share of total retailing volume of chains is at an all-time high with more than 62 percent. Once again, this indicates a concentration of economic power in the hands of fewer and fewer chains.

To further reinforce the above observation, it can be stated that independents in retailing account for 84.2 percent of all retail establishments. However, their market share is at an all-time low with a 37.9 percent share of all of retail sales. Perhaps this fact reinforces the presence of a retail jungle where small independent retailers find it more and more difficult to survive.

The era of independent large-scale retailing catering to middle class consumers appears to be somewhat gone. While in 1972 department stores accounted for 13.6 percent of total retail sales, this proportion has gone down to less than 10 percent in 1997. This is partially due to the declining middle class in America. Additionally, discounting has been pushing its competitive edge and luring department store customers. Thus, large department stores are being replaced by discount chains.

It is critical for a retailer to detect trends in society. Although these trends can be a threat, they can also be great opportunities. The trends that are cited here have been playing a profound role in how retailing is conducted for the new retail population. It is clear that they are sending a message to small retailers directly. The message is: *you must do a better job in creating customer value if you want to survive in this jungle.* If we want to create greater customer value, we must have a clear idea about consumer trends.

RECENT CONSUMER TRENDS

Developments among consumers in recent times have had quite an impact on retailing. These changes have largely centered around the flowering of cyberspace, changing lifestyles that have become evident, changes in consumer demographics, increasing retail competition including more and more e-tailing, and growth in international retailing. These topics will be covered now.

Development of Cyberspace

Perhaps the most profound trend during the past decade has been the utilization of cyberspace by the retailing sector. As stated earlier, some retailers went overboard by emphasizing cyberspace—clicks as opposed to bricks. They closed down their stores and went into e-tailing, a strategy which backfired. They lost much money, and some of them, their existence. They failed. However, some retailers have taken the middle road in coping with this trend. They have pursued a multimedia approach to retail promotion, a strategy which is discussed in Chapter 10 of this book.

Changing Lifestyles

In a dynamic market system such as ours, consumers' lifestyles change quite regularly. These changes are reflected in the retailing sector almost as quickly as they emerge. During the past decade or so, American consumers displayed a number of consumption trends, including the desire for low-fat and low-carb products, health food supplements, bottled water, casual apparel, computer games, and home improvement supplies. This list could go on much longer. Naturally, detecting these trends early would give the retailers "the first mover advantage." But looking at the big picture, retailers who do not follow changing lifestyles and swiftly cater to these trends do not do well in the market.

Consumer Demographics

American society is growing older. Baby boomers are becoming the fifty-plus group. The older and faster growing segments have reasonable amounts of money and are going for more sporty cars, travel, and entertainment. Facilities for assisted living are expanding, along with demand for pharmaceuticals and other health care activities.

Increasing Retail Competition

As discussed in the previous chapter, retail competition is increasing. As this happens, consumers expect new products, new services, and greater values. Thus, some retailers are responding to changing consumer expectations and, hence, numerous changes are taking place in retailing to improve consumer values. These changes are creating more competition in the retailing sector.

More E-tailing

The attachment of the American consumer to TV provided the genesis of telemarketing, a trend which subsequently is giving way to e-tailing. There are more consumers who like to play with their computers rather than shop. E-tailing is getting its impetus from these consumers. Furthermore, as mentioned earlier, the older consumer market is growing fast, and both telemarketing and e-tailing are preferred by this group, since some of these consumers are not very mobile and haven't the energy to shop physically.

International Retailing

During the past decade or so, many developments in the direction of internationalization of American retailing have taken place. Not only have foreign-owned retail establishments such as IKEA and Benetton flourished, many nonAmerican brands have also become popular. Furthermore, many nonbranded items, particularly in the apparel sector, have been imported and branded in the United States for sale. Certainly, such activities broadened the choice of American consumers in terms of selection as well as price.

In exploring recent trends in the retail population, one must also analyze certain key economic factors that have impacted directly as well as indirectly on that population.

CRITICAL ECONOMIC TRENDS

Numerous critical trends have emerged in the overall economic setting within which the retailing sector functions. Among these are business cycles, changing consumer profiles, and political environment.

Business Cycles

Small retailers, perhaps more than any other type of business, suffer from business cycles. On the average, over 50,000 businesses go out of existence yearly. Most of these failures are caused not so much by managerial missteps as by adversities in the economy. Along with an increase in the number of business failures during recessions comes an increase in the number of small retailers. This is because many people laid off because of the recession try to establish their own businesses. Because many of them are not properly prepared to own and run their stores, they fail in a short period of time. These failures are costly not only to individuals who are closely related to the failed entrepreneurs, but to the economy as well.

There are no guarantees for survival, but it is possible to develop a counter business cycle strategy for these small and vulnerable retailers. Some of these countercyclical measures are discussed in different parts of this book. Suffice it to say here that in recessions small businesses must be able to adjust their retail mixes. Lower-priced product mixes with more classical and traditional lines, coupled with lower prices and increased promotion, are necessary ingredients of counterrecession strategies. At no time can small retailers afford to lower the service they deliver by laying off their employees, or cut costs by reducing promotion, or charge more for products. Such practices would prove to be detrimental for the retail establishment.

Changing Consumer Profiles

As mentioned earlier, income distribution in the United States has been changing somewhat in favor of upper income groups. During the past two decades or so, incomes of the upper fifth of the population have increased substantially while the middle two fifths remained about the same and the lowest fifth of the population have falling incomes. although during the late 1990s this pattern somewhat reversed itself, department stores appealing to the middle class have had a very difficult time and a number of them have failed. Discount stores and other low-price variety stores such as category killers have become quite successful. As mentioned earlier, large-scale wholesale buying clubs also benefited from this trend. At the writing of this book, there has been a large sum of tax reduction introduced along with a rather heavy emphasis on upper income. While Kmart or Wal-Mart may not benefit from this tax cut, retailers catering to upper income consumers are likely to.

Political Environment

Although strictly speaking not an economic factor, the political environment has had a secondary impact on the retail population. More lenient bankruptcy laws and changes to the tax code which give some consumer groups more spending money while limiting the spending activity of others always create changes in the retail population. Many small businesses, because of the leniency of the bankruptcy laws, did go bankrupt. As the code became more lopsided by providing more income for the upper income class, retail establishments with high status received a boost. Similarly, availability of credit and lending activities of organizations such as the Small Business Administration have had their impact as well on the changing retail population.

Thus retailers, particularly small-scale retailers, are influenced by many trends in the economy, specifically the local economy. These trends may help or hinder their activities. It is critical for a retailer to spot these trends, understand their implications, and use them to advantage. Survival for a retailer is the manipulation of probabilities. The higher the probability of success, the better off the retail establishment. Managing the trends influencing the survival of the retail establishment is a must. Without such management, the chances for survival quickly fall. Small-scale retailing always faces a greater risk than larger-scale retail establishments and chains. This is so because such establishments do not have large financial resources on which to rely in times of hardship. Hence, small retailers need to pay attention to trends, particularly the trickle effects of national trends on the local economy. As was mentioned earlier, they may be even more influenced by local developments than by the trickle-down effects of national trends. However, national trends also play a critical role. A small retailer may find himself contrasting the relative importance of local events as opposed to national trends. It is not an exaggeration to state that the small retailer needs to be a practical combination of sociologist, economist, and political scientist.

THE "E" REVOLUTION

Although it will be touched upon throughout the book as needed, it is important to consider the "E" revolution as one of the major trends profoundly influencing the retailing sector. By enhancing storage and transmission of data, information technology (IT) enhanced the emergence of more efficient markets, better access to data, improved local, national, and global communication, and more (Strauss, El-Ansary and Frost 2003). IT, as part of total information systems (IS), is used readily by national or international retailing giants for competitive reasons. IT and IS provide very important advantages over the traditional systems by creating, among other advantages, compelling logistics efficiencies. The retailing giants are locked in competition with each other and, hence, any cost-saving and decision-making tools that IT provides are not only beneficial but necessary.

However, small and medium-sized retailers can and indeed should use IT and IS, not because they are competing with retailing giants but because they want to improve their own operating efficiencies to provide better service to their identified target markets. IT and IS enable them to customize their merchandise mixes and their service offerings. If, for example, they have better information about their markets and the movement of their inventory and, accordingly, if they can improve their inventory replenishment process, they will be able to provide a better choice to their customers more swiftly and accurately.

At the writing of this book, a new concept in IT coined Radio Frequency Identification (RFID) is in the process of emerging. RFID has tags inserted in every product to identify and track items from the time they leave the factory until they reach the consumer's home and, if necessary, beyond. Although RFID raises many concerns about privacy of the individual, it could also provide very important information for the retailer. It remains to be seen how RFID is going to be used (<u>Supermarket Guru</u>, July 2003).

SUMMARY

Retail populations change. Exhibit 3-2 shows key groups of trends influence this change: Recent retailing trends, organizational trends, consumer trends, and economic trends. It is critical to reiterate that any retailer must have a reasonable understanding of these externalities that sometimes can be rather unfriendly. The retailer must manage these trends. Managing them implies recognizing, understanding, and acting (or counteracting). By managing these trends successfully, the retailer establishes a competitive advantage which, in turn, generates customer value.

Exhibit 3-2. Influences on Retail Population

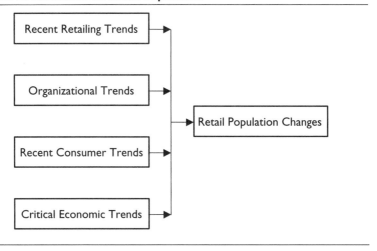

REFERENCES

Berman, Barry, and Evans, Joel R. (2002), *Retail Management*, Upper Saddle River, NJ: Prentice Hall.

Strauss, Judy, El-Ansary, Adel, and Frost, Raymond (2003). *E-Marketing*, Upper Saddle River, NJ: Prentice Hall.

Supermarket Guru (2003), "Quick Poll Results," July 11, 1–3.

The Retail Evolution

I f we don't know how we got here, it will be hard to decide the best way to go next. Not knowing the nature of the evolution that took place in the retail sector of this country makes it almost impossible for a new retailer to function. Just what may be expected to be the far-reaching impact of developments in retailing? How these changes are likely to touch our particular business must be constant concerns on which to ponder.

Retailing takes place in specific places according to population movements and resultant population concentrations. It must be reiterated that in our market economy, unless they generate consumer value, retail establishments cannot survive. This survival is dependent on offering products and services in close proximity to consumers so that they do not need to travel long distances to search for those goods and services they need and that, above all, they desire.

The retailing sector has been generating consumer value in three distinct ways simultaneously. By being accessible, by providing the necessary goods and services, and by grouping with other retailers that complement the total offering, retailers in the United States have managed well. This process of generating consumer value has been evolutionary, and the evolution continues.

RETAIL EVOLUTION

In order to follow the evolutionary movement of the retailing sector, it is necessary to observe the institutions and their locations. This observation must be, at least loosely, to some extent a chronological analysis.

The American population is very mobile. As it moves, rather noticeably, the retailing sector tries to accommodate by moving in the same direction and maintaining a high level of accessibility. Retail evolution, first and foremost, needs to be analyzed in terms of the type of stores responding to population movements.

Retailing in the United States started primarily with general stores. The population was more rural than urban, and these stores had all the basic necessities from food to weapons and medication. The products were not standardized, categorized, or packaged. But they were available. Almost simultaneously, owner-operated small retail stores emerged and grouped in the heart of population centers. This was the beginning of downtowns.

The need for more specialized, more personal, and more convenient stores, particularly in rural population centers, led to the emergence of "Mom and Pop" stores.

When urban population concentration became substantial, department stores started emerging. They dominated American retailing for a long while.

As urban populations started moving to the suburbs, shopping centers emerged. Retailing had to be close to the lucrative markets of suburbia.

Because of climactic extremes, shopping centers in some parts of the country gave way to enclosed shopping malls. Providing the consumer with a comfortable atmosphere appeared to be working, again, mostly in the suburbs.

Downtowns responded with specialized small, elegant boutiques and specialty stores that make consumers come back to downtowns and make their shopping experiences exciting and colorful.

As the population became more and more dispersed, retailing also became dispersed, with convenience stores, ice cream parlors, small pizzerias, and video stores, to name but a few types of shops. Exhibit 4-1 illustrates this approximately 100-year evolution. Retailing, while trying to reach out and stay in close proximity to the population, also tries to steal populations from other towns, cities, and population centers. If and when consumers are not satisfied with the existing retailing facilities in their town, and when very attractive retail facilities are bunched up out of town, consumers go outshopping.

OUTSHOPPING

Outshopping, or intermarket shopping, is a critical phenomenon every retailer must understand. Those located in small rural areas must be particularly sensitive to outshopping tendencies and processes. As mentioned earlier, location is the lifeblood of retailing. Two key principles move retailers in location decisions. First,

Exhibit 4-1. Retail Evolution and Population Pressure

INSTITUTION	POPULATION PRESSURE
General Stores	Scattered semi-rural populations
Traditional Retail Stores	In population centers, satisfying the need for specialized merchandise
Mom and Pop Stores	Concentrated population, convenience seeking
Department Stores	Urban population concentrated in downtowns
Shopping Centers	Suburbanization of populations
Malls	Accommodating consumers by modifying the climate
Boutiques	Special needs of well-off consumers
Convenience Stores	Suburban population centers and major traffic routes access

retailers must follow the population to get as close to their customers or prospective customers as possible. Second, retailers, by grouping together and promoting jointly, motivate their customers and try to bring them to the specific location in question. Even though these two principles may seem to be opposing each other, they are actually complementary. This means that while retailers need to locate conveniently vis-à-vis their customers, they also expect certain groups of people to move towards different shopping complexes. Such movements among different shopping complexes can render the current location of the retailers as "good," "questionable," or "bad."

In some cases, consumers travel from one urban complex or suburban complex to another. This means they go out of the area or out of town to shop. Understanding the intermarket shopping patterns is important for a retailer as part of the self-preservation instinct. As populations become more mobile and as communications about retailing opportunities for consumers become more available, intermarket mobility for retailing purposes has become rather powerful. This phenomenon is an important part of American retailing evolution and is likely to continue and expand in different ways.

A MODEL OF INTERMARKET SHOPPING

Particularly in relatively isolated small towns, somewhat isolated communities, or in dormitory areas where people live but work and shop elsewhere, retailers must know to what extent consumers are leaving the area to shop. Exhibit 4-2 presents a model for intermarket purchase behavior.

The model revolves around the needs and wants of consumers, how they emerge and how they are taken care of. Consumers' needs and wants are generated, stimulated, or modified by their lifestyle. This, in turn, is formed by the level of their education and their degree of sophistication. Their background is also part of this equation and relates to their degree of sophistication. If consumers have refined needs and wants that local retailing facilities cannot satisfy, then consumers are likely to outshop. Where they go is partially based on their loyalty to the town or area where they live, as well as on the attractiveness of other shopping facilities in other towns or cities. However, distance is always a deterrent, which can be partially overcome by strong promotional activity from other shopping complexes. Some consumers from southwest Virginia may fly out to the D.C. area or to New York occasionally for shopping because these shopping facilities are extensively advertised and offer tremendous varieties. For small communities with retailers who are not sensitive enough or do not understand the needs of consumers and their behavior patterns, intermarket purchasing of this type could be borderline devastating. Small communities experiencing much outshopping cannot generate enough income to develop the community further, and shopping facilities remain underdeveloped in that they cannot satisfy the needs of more demanding groups in the community. Intermarket shopping goes on in significant proportions, particularly in rural communities that are

Exhibit 4-2. A General Model of Intermarket Purchase Behavior

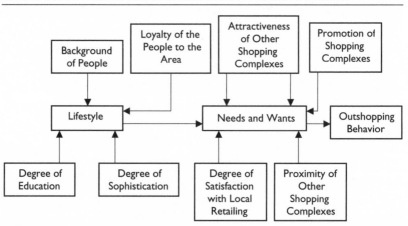

located near major cities with large-scale shopping facilities or regional shopping centers.

Intermarket shopping behavior can be particularly critical when, for instance, Wal-Mart and a few other stores establish an attractive and modern regional shopping center out of town or out of the area. In such cases the regular retailers of the area must search for better communications with their current customers, improved service, and a substantially improved merchandise mix and pricing structure that they are willing to offer these customers.

In recent years, retail evolution has taken the industry to a higher plateau, which is e-tailing. Some consumers do not like to shop around, while some others are insufficiently mobile. In both cases, they can buy almost anything they wish to buy from anywhere in the world by using the Internet. This is discussed further in this chapter. Suffice it to say that outshopping, including e-tail, must be counteracted by the retailer for survival. One aspect of evolution, mentioned earlier, must be given special attention here. As the population spreads out to suburbs, retailing emphasis moves away from downtown to shopping centers and further to local clusters.

FROM DOWNTOWN TO SHOPPING CENTERS

As society changes, consumer behavior also is modified, if not completely changed. Retail competition is expected to react to these changes and accommodate them. During the past three decades or so, downtowns throughout the country have experienced difficult times. First, emerging shopping centers encourage outshopping and take customers away from downtowns or central business districts (CBDs). Second, CBDs appear to be suffering from lack of vision and competitive creativity. Many downtowns' stores have been there for a long time and have done the same things year in and year out. Therefore, they may be suffering from an acute case of inertia. In recent years, most American downtowns have been under pressure to do something to reverse their declining profitability and appeal.

Five specific reasons may explain the plight of downtowns. These are population dispersion, uncoordinated marketing, emergence of shopping centers, decreasing accessibility, and inertia.

Population Dispersion

Perhaps one-fifth of the American population moves every year. In such a dynamic society, it is natural to expect major trends in population movement. Among these are exoduses from the Northeast to the Southwest and from the Midwest to the Southeast. But perhaps the most important population movement has been from cities to suburbs. Thus the population is not only mobile, but dispersing as well. As markets are dispersing, it is becoming difficult for the retailer to keep abreast of the population movement patterns and to satisfy consumer needs. Such movements have particularly been adversely affecting downtown retailing complexes.

Uncoordinated Marketing

Downtown retailing complexes are typically composed of many independent entrepreneurs, who own their stores and run their businesses independently. This is one of the key problems of CBDs. Downtowns need coordinated marketing and merchandising efforts, yet businesses are varied without any patterns, their promotional efforts are not coordinated, and they do not collaborate with other merchants. Thus, CBDs not only have lacked synergism, but also have moved rather aimlessly. For instance, coordinated special sales, advertising, or special effects could bring about a synergistic impact, which is rarely experienced in downtowns.

Emerging Shopping Centers

During the past half century or so, retailing's response to population dispersion has been the emergence of shopping centers. Planned shopping centers are the antithesis of central business districts. They emerged as American suburbia mushroomed. This retailing phenomenon first came into existence in the early 1950s. Unlike downtowns, shopping centers displayed five important features that make them successful. First, these shopping complexes are very accessible for the consumers who are tired of crowded downtowns and the traffic snags that make it difficult to shop. Second, they were—and some still are—modern and well-planned facilities that provide extensive one-stop shopping for more mobile and discriminating consumers who live in suburbia or come from downtowns. Third, parking is simple and easy. All shopping centers are surrounded by adequate parking facilities that cannot be compared to the crowded conditions of downtown shopping complexes. Fourth, they pursue coordinated merchandising and marketing activities of the whole complex. Fifth and finally, shopping centers present general themes and architecture that make them unique and attractive.

Decreasing Accessibility

As the car population increases on our highways, the roads do not increase and improve proportionately, and traffic, particularly in downtowns, becomes difficult to cope with. Naturally, access to shopping becomes progressively worse. This pattern has been going on for four or five decades. Hence, not only are people fleeing the downtowns, but businesses are also either closing down or moving away.

Inertia

The type of inertia that is particularly related to the practices of retailers in downtowns has been going on for a long time. Many of these businesses did not know how to change and improve their business practices. As market conditions become adverse, many retailers did not have the capability to cope with emerging adversities.

As a result of these five negative factors, downtowns throughout the country are in some degree of trouble. The conditions are likely to get still worse before they get better. Considering the fact that the population is growing, available land downtown is not increasing, and many CBDs are no longer very functional, it is necessary to address these issues. Many downtown development plans have taken place, and many more are needed. Experience has shown that rejuvenation of downtowns is by no means automatic and indeed in many cases is almost impossible. However, as population increases, space in suburbia becomes more limited, and suburban shopping centers become older, there may be a dramatic rejuvenation of downtowns in the coming decades.

The next stage of evolution in Exhibit 4-1 encompasses the malls. A major trend in retailing has been the emergence of malls and movement from malls to local clusters.

FROM MALLS TO LOCAL CLUSTERS

As shopping centers emerged, they also started competing with each other. One of the most logical ways of competing was by controlling atmospheres. This led to the emergence of enclosed shopping malls. In time, malls also started competing among themselves in terms of design, merchant mix, quality, and service, as well as through other promotional activities such as concerts, art displays, and the like. Most of the malls are large and somewhat equal to regional shopping centers. But, as population continued dispersing further away from suburbs, it became necessary to have shopping centers more conveniently located for local consumers. Consequently, there emerged three new retailing complexes: community shopping centers, neighborhood shopping centers, and neighborhood clusters.

Exhibit 4-3 on pages 46–47 illustrates their features and contrasts these three relatively new retailing complexes with each other and the with regional shopping centers. As can be seen, the closer the retail facility gets to consumers, the more it concentrates on convenience products and services. Similarly, regional shopping centers, in particular, emphasize many specialty goods such as select gift items and more expensive shopping goods such as appliances, furniture, apparel, and the like.

It must be restated that the further away the retail complex gets from consumers, the more planning is necessary regarding the overall theme, promotional strategies, and merchandise and service mixes, among others.

Neighborhood clusters are probably the most active retail complexes. By definition, they follow emerging new construction activity. They are typically composed of a convenience store, ice cream parlor, video shop, bicycle repair shop, barber shop, and the like. They need to be very close to consumers and provide as much convenience as possible. One aspect of these different retail facilities needs to be further explored, and that is is their use of cyberspace.

FROM BRICKS TO CLICKS

The emergence of e-trade or e-tail activity came along very suddenly and almost as a shock. As mentioned earlier, in Chapter 3, many retailers treated cyberspace as a total market with its own demand and supply, and with its own communication and delivery system. These retailers went completely away from "bricks" to "clicks." They closed down their businesses and went on-line exclusively. This was not the best alternative. Almost none of the exclusive clickers survived.

A second alternative was to treat cyberspace as a distribution channel. Many retailers reduced their bricking activities in favor of clicking. Once again, this did not enhance their retailing position. They could not promote sales and deliver merchandise. Many more ceased to exist.

The third alternative was to treat cyberspace as a communication channel, a supplement to existing communication activity. These retailers simply added the Internet to their communications mix. Unlike the first two groups above, this third group has done and is still doing quite well. Almost all of the sound names in retailing have developed their Internet capabilities and are accessible for e-trading. They combine multiple channels. They receive orders online that are to be picked up at a physical store, thus reducing the waiting time for delivery and still providing shopping convenience. Being a well-known bricker and adding clicking capabilities, at this point in time, appears to be a positive development in the never-ending retail evolution.

ENTER THE INTERNATIONAL DIMENSION

In addition to population dispersion, during the past two decades or so, retailing has also followed buying power around the world. Hence, international retailing has been mushrooming. In addition to international chains such as IKEA, Benetton's, McDonald's, and KFC, many retailers such as Kmart and Wal-Mart started importing a large variety of products in large quantities. Although in this book we do not deal with the international dimension to a great extent, we will make reference to it as needed. It is clear that the international dimension of retailing is likely to develop further and, indeed, even accelerate its development. Here, again, retailing will follow the population, particularly the population with particular needs and buying power.

FOLLOWING THE POPULATION DISPERSION

The retailing sector in the United States has primarily been following the population. Unlike a century or half a century ago, the retailing sector is not trying to lead the population but is following it. The last step in this process of following the population

Exhibit 4-3. From Shopping Centers to Local Clusters

	TYPES OF SHOPPING COMPLEXES			
FEATURES	REGIONAL SHOPPING CENTERS	COMMUNITY SHOPPING CENTERS	NEIGHBORHOOD SHOPPING CENTERS	NEIGHBORHOOD CLUSTERS
Location	Outside central city at the edge of town or major expressway network	Close to populated residential areas (preferably more than one)	Along a major thoroughfare in one residential area	A group of stores in a residential area
Proximity	30 minutes or more driving time	15 to 20 minutes driving time	5 to 10 minutes driving time	3-5 minutes walking distance
Economic base necessary to support the facility in terms of number people in the area	100,000	20,000 to 100,000	3,000 to 20,000	3,000 or less
Size in square feet rented to various retailers	400,000 to 2,000,000+	100,000 to 400,000	30,000 to 100,000	Less than 30,000
Number of stores	50-150+	15 to 50	10 to 15	Less than 10

Goods and services mix	Very large assortment of shopping and specialty goods; specialty services that should enhance the shopping experience	Moderate assortment of shopping and convenience goods and services	Limited assortment of convenience goods and services with some shopping goods	Total emphasis is on convenience and basic goods and services
Principal tenant	One, two, or more full-sized traditional department stores	One discount department store and/or category killer store	Supermarket or drugstore or both	No principal tenant, a convenience store, bakery, barbershop, etc.
Layout	Mall, often enclosed with anchorstores at major entrances	Strip or L-shaped	Strip	Just a group of stores
Planning status	Always carefully planned	Carefully planned with some unplanned features	Some planning with much unplanned activity	Barely planned
E-trade capabilities	Some to good	Fair	Little	None

Source: Adapted and revised from Samli; 1998.

is e-trading. Since it is almost impossible to reach out everywhere, retailers will use the Internet to further promote themselves, their merchandise, and their services. This is in place of a physical presence in certain areas. However, as these locations develop further in terms of a necessary population density, they will require the retailer's physical presence. As discussed in different parts of this book, cyberspace cannot possibly *replace* retailing. The presence of retailing facilities appeals to many consumer needs, and these facilities create much additional consumer value.

LOCATION, LOCATION, LOCATION

Throughout this chapter, the location theme has been repeated. Retailing not only follows the population dispersion, but also locates convenient to certain population groups. It must be stated forcefully that location is the first lifeblood of retailing. No matter how good, how attractive, or how accommodating, if a retailer is not located properly, there is no possibility of his or her establishment's success.

SUMMARY

The evolutionary nature of retailing has been explored in this chapter. Through time the physical facility of retailing has changed from general country store to shopping centers, malls, and discount stores. It is important to realize that all of these changes are almost a direct response to a changing and more demanding population.

As the population dispersed from traditional urban centers, regional shopping centers, neighborhood shopping centers, and neighborhood clusters emerged. If retailing cannot physically reach consumers, it can resort to e-tailing. However, location is emphasized as the lifeblood of retailing. Close proximity and accessibility are necessary outcomes of retail location. Without proximity and accessibility, retailing cannot be in a position to satisfy consumer needs and create consumer value. The chapter presents a comparative analysis of different types of shopping centers and neighborhood clusters. Small retailers must know where they belong and what to emphasize, so that they can survive the retail jungle.

5

Capitalizing on
Market Potentials

If the macro and micro conditions are favorable, then the retailer should go ahead and start the business. But it must be remembered that approximately 30 percent of new retail establishments survive less than six months. At least three preliminary activities should be conducted to indicate that macro and micro conditions are all favorable for the proposed retail establishment to start. These three preliminary activities proposed here are the following: assessing market potentials, evaluating the feasibility of the proposed retail establishment, and determining the capital needs of the proposed store.

GEOGRAPHIC DIMENSIONS
AND MARKET POTENTIALS

Since retail location is not a very flexible activity after a store is located, it is important to connect the proposed location to market potentials before the location decision is carefully studied and finalized. Once the location decision is made, it will be difficult to change or modify it. Hence, the decision must be made carefully in advance.

Preliminary location analysis must guide us in the direction of making concrete location decisions. These preliminary analyzes must include (1) choosing the approximate location, (2) assessing the area's growth and actual potential, and (3) evaluating that area's *retail saturation level.*

Unlike major retail chains, an independent retailer-to-be is not likely to choose the most dynamic city in the country in which to locate a store. In other words, small retailers seldom undertake careful and objective analysis of location options. Typically an independent retailer-to-be goes with familiarity rather than solid economic criteria for the first line of decision, choosing approximately where to locate.

All national chains, such as International House of Pancakes, Kroger, or Eckerd, employ formulas regarding the opening of a new store. Unless the conditions in the formula are satisfied, they will not move to a new location. These conditions include such items as growth, base population, competition, and the like. Thus, the location decisions for major national or international retailers are rather scientific and are designed to reduce risk and enhance profitability.

An independent retailer-to-be faces a different problem. The chances are that the general area where the store may be located is likely to be based, somewhat arbitrarily, on the familiarity of that retailer-to-be. However, even if it is not a very common practice, this does not mean the choice of approximate location should not go through a rigorous analysis.

Exhibit 5-1 illustrates a seven-step complete analysis before a store becomes a real entity. Identifying the particular area, which may be a whole town as opposed to the neighboring town or two, is the critical first step. This can be accomplished in a number of different ways. Four such approaches are briefly discussed here: buying power index, percentage of expenditures, special bottom-up, and geographic information systems (GIS).

Exhibits 5-2, 5-3, 5-4 and 5-5 deal with these four approaches. Exhibit 5-2 provides the Sales and Marketing Management

Exhibit 5-1. Assessing Market Potential and Capital Needs

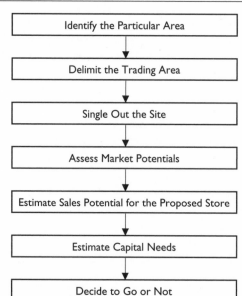

Identify the Particular Area

↓

Delimit the Trading Area

↓

Single Out the Site

↓

Assess Market Potentials

↓

Estimate Sales Potential for the Proposed Store

↓

Estimate Capital Needs

↓

Decide to Go or Not

Exhibit 5-2. The Use of Buying Power Index[a]

Income[b]	$1.1 \cdot 5 = 5.5$
Retail Sales[c]	$0.4 \cdot 3 = 1.2$
Population[d]	$\underline{0.5 \cdot 2 = 1.0}$
	$7.7 \div 10 = 0.77$

[a]Hypothetical figures
[b]Income as a percentage of national total
[c]Retail Sales as a percentage of national income
[d]Population as a percent of national total

buying power index. *Sales and Marketing Management Journal* has been presenting a buying power index (BPI) for more than four decades. This index is based on three key criteria: income, retail sales, and population, weighted by 5, 3 and 2, respectively, which expresses the locality's buying power as a percent of national total. The Exhibit 5-2 calculation indicates that the area in question has about .77 percent of the national total. If there are $2 billion of auto tires sold in the country, .77 percent will be sold in the area under study. In general terms, BPI is used to approximate market potential in the area for any and all products as a percent of the national total.

Exhibits 5-3 and 5-4 display total expenditures in a specified area for a specific product line. By establishing incomes of different income categories and connecting them to national average expenditures in each category for that product category, it becomes possible to determine how much will be spent on the consumption category that is being analyzed in the area of study. This is a top-down approach that is utilized often, particularly by larger retailers. It is more macro and can provide a more general evaluation of market opportunities.

Exhibit 5-3. District of Jacosonville, Florida, and National Distribution of Expenditures on Food

INCOME PER HOUSEHOLD	PERCENTAGE OF ALL HOUSEHOLD	TOTAL PERCENTAGE OF EXPENDITURES ON FOOD IN U.S.
$10,000–14,999	5.2	23.9
$15,000–24,999	12.1	21.0
$25,000–49,999	31.3	10.6
$50,000 & Over	44.0	8.0

Source: Department of Commerce (2002), U.S. Department of Labor (2002)
Note: Total number of households in Jacksonville was 425,525 as of November 6, 2002

Exhibit 5-4. Estimated Total Personal Income, Number of Households in Each Income Category, and Estimated Expenditures on Food, Jacksonville, Florida

INCOME PER HOUSEHOLD	NUMBER OF UNITS[a]	TOTAL ESTIMATED INCOME[b]	TOTAL ESTIMATED EXPENDITURES OF FOOD[c]
$10,000-14,999	22,127	276,591,250.00	66,105,309.00
$15,000-24,999	51,489	1,029,770,500.00	216,251,805.00
$25,000-49,999	133,189	4,994,599,687.50	529,427,566.88
$50,000 & Over	187,231	17,786,645,000.00	1,422,955,600.00

[a]Estimates are based on household percentages in Exhibit 5-3 multiplied by the total number of households.

[b]Number of units were multiplied by the midpoint of income per household, with the exception of the last category, in which an estimated average income of 95,000 was utilized.

[c]Total income figures were multiplied by total percentage of expenditure figures in Exhibit 5-3.

A special bottom-up approach is displayed in Exhibit 5-5. Unlike the first two, this is a strictly micro approach. Small retailers are more in need of micro or bottom-up orientation. This is because small retailers are more closely bound by specific location, and the overall market conditions are not the same at all sites. This approach can be used more readily for certain circumstances such as the one displayed in Exhibit 5-5. In this exhibit, the market potential is derived from the number of automobiles, which can be estimated from the number of cars per

Exhibit 5-5. Estimating Market Potential For a Service Station

Steps

1. Number of automobiles in the specified area = 50,000
2. Number of service stations in the specified area = 50
3. Average number of cars per service station

$$\frac{Number\ of\ autos}{Number\ of\ Service\ Stations} = \frac{50,000}{50} = 1,000\ cars\ per\ station$$

4. Cost associated with car maintenance and operation (including gas, oil, and service):

   Cost of driving one mile = $0.55
   Average mileage driven per year = 12,000
   Cost of driving one mile • average mileage driven per year:

   $0.55 • 12,000 = $6,600 per car including services

5. Cost per car times average number of cars 6,600 • $1,000 = $6,600,000, on the average $6.6 million volume per service station.

person nationally and the number of people in the study area. As one might speculate, certain sites for a service station may be evaluated by location conditions regarding vehicular traffic.

In recent years, computerized data systems have become available which can be used for location decisions. The Geographic Information System is one such example. This System is very versatile. It is a more expanded version of the percentage of expenditures approach. It can give the demographics of specific areas and can combine the demographics with expenditures on a variety of products and services. All of these approaches help to clarify retailing opportunities.

DELIMITING THE TRADING AREA

The attempt to determine the area retail potential would lead in the direction of delimiting the trading area for a particular store in a given location. Geographic delineation of an area containing potential customers for a prospective retailer or a retailing complex, such as a shopping center, is critical. Only by such delineation can the feasibility of the proposed retail establishment or the retailing complex be established. This delineated geographic area is called the retail trading area (Samli 1998). Ideally, the trading area would minimize the cost of contact between consumers and retailers. It basically implies that as retailers have the greatest access to the market with the most potential, the possibility of creating the most consumer value becomes real because consumers also will have the greatest access to the best retailing facility based on their perception.

Samli (1998) maintains that identification of a retail trading area is based on three sets of analysis.

1. Is there a critical mass of population that is likely to be patronizing the proposed retailing facility?
2. What is the proportion of the critical mass that lives in the immediate area? For example, if 55–70 percent of the prospective customers live in that area, they will be identified as the primary trading area. If 15–25 percent of the prospective customers are located in the area, they will be identified as the secondary trading area. The remainder of the market may be identified as the fringe trading area.
3. What is the proportion of the purchases that will take place in the proposed retailing facility? Just what is the proposed retailing facility's competitive advantage?

These three points must be operationalized. However, additional information regarding (1) the demographic and socioeconomic characteristics of the prospective customers in the area, (2) the future growth or decline potential of the area, and (3) the number of stores that the area can possibly support without becoming overcrowded by retail stores must also be calculated.

Obviously, a prospective new store's trading area is not based on current patronage but on some evaluation of market opportunities. Samli (1998) states that the proportion of the store's total sales establishes the variations in the trading area. The primary trading area may be the people who live in the geographic core from which a store obtains about 55 to 70 percent of its business. This is followed by the secondary trading area from which the store gets between 15 and 25 percent of its business. A tertiary area can be added to the first two that would account for 5 to 10 percent of the store's business. The remainder of the trading area may yield about 5 percent of the total business. There may also be a fringe to the whole of the trading area with somewhere around 2 percent or less, based on some unexpected sales from various remote areas.

As was stated earlier, proximity is typically construed as the trading area's determining factor, which may be expressed in terms of distance and time (both in terms of driving and walking time). Here the objective criteria of the number of people or the number of households with the average income and proportion of spending on that type of business (e.g., groceries, apparel, etc.) would give the first line of estimations. It must be reiterated that this first line of estimations is a joint product of census tracts that give information that is related to housing units, number of people, income, education and other basic information, and the Bureau of Labor Statistics. The latter gives information regarding what proportion of income is spent on which general product categories by different income groups. By combining census tract data and Bureau of Labor Statistics, estimates can be generated about the market potential in the geographic area. This is deemed as part of the trading area expressed in census tracts (Exhibit 5-2).

The objective criteria must be supplemented by outshopping tendencies, which are approximated in at least three different subjective ways: questionnaires, traveling distance preferences, and Internet or e-trade involvement.

Questionnaires: Using survey techniques to determine the extent to which individuals are typically committed to buying in the area versus going out of the area (outshopping) is not new. In such attempts, determining the tendency for outshopping indirectly is important. Instead of asking prospective customers if they will go to Areas X, Y, Z, it is better to find out where, when, and how much they have purchased of the product or the service categories in question.

Traveling Distance Preferences: This particular dimension has two key parts—the impact of retail gravitation, and concentric circles. As early as the 1930s, Reilly developed the retail gravitation hypothesis. It was based on the premise that two cities attract consumers for retail trade from any intermediate city or town in direct proportion to the population of the two cities in question and in inverse proportion to the square of the distances from the intermediate city or town to either one of the two cities. Based on this hypothesis (or Reilly's Law), it is possible to locate a retailing facility most optimally between the two cities. Assume, for example, that two cities, A and B, have populations of 100,000 and 900,000, respectively. The distance between the two is 80 miles. If we want to locate a regional shopping center between the two cities in an optimal location, according to Reilly's Law, the following formula will be used.

The optimal location between A and B $= \dfrac{\text{miles between A and B}}{1+\sqrt{\dfrac{\text{population of B}}{\text{population of A}}}}$

Based on the above given data:

$$Bb = \frac{80}{1+\sqrt{\dfrac{900,000}{100,000}}} = \frac{80}{1+\sqrt{9}} = \frac{80}{1+3} = \frac{80}{4} = 20, \quad Bb = \text{breaking point from B}$$

Thus, the optimal location for the proposed regional shopping center between A and B is 20 miles out of A and 60 miles out of B. Because of the fact that B has four times the drawing power of A, by locating 60 miles out of B, the drawing power of the two cities is equalized, and the location of the proposed shopping complex will be optimized without favoring one or the other of the two cities. This is also known as the breaking point or point of indifference.

A revision of the retail gravitation model has dealt with substituting square footage of each retailer for population and further substituting the actual travel time to these cities for the distance between cities (Samli 1998). These substitutions make sense. First, substituting the square footage for population implies that larger square footage means greater variety and choice. This means drawing power. Second, actual travel time as opposed to distance implies that accessibility of the retail complex is more critical in terms of time spent to reach the retail facility. A comparison between two retailing complexes will illustrate. Retailing Complex A is located about 5 miles distant, but there are about 25 traffic lights to cross. Retailing Complex B is located about 10 miles distant, but there are no traffic lights. Complex B is likely to be preferred because of the time spent to get there.

Accessibility and travel time to the shopping facility have triggered the additional concept of concentric circles. By drawing concentric circles indicating, for example, 5-minute, 10-minute, or 15-minute driving distances around the proposed approximate location of the new retail facility, it becomes possible to establish what kind of a market potential the new proposed facility possesses and how much of it may be taken away by the already existing competition.

E-trade or the Internet Involvement: For the shopper who prefers to use the computer for shopping activity, the trading area becomes the whole world, meaning that a shopper can buy virtually anything from anywhere in the world. Although e-trading has expanded substantially during the past decade, this author believes that it will not amount to more than about 10 percent of total retail volume due to the fact that the real retail shopping experience is substantially more interesting than virtual shopping. However, 10 percent of total retail dollar volume is not something to ignore. This is a very large sum, and it is almost essential that all retailers participate. This is discussed further in Chapter 10.

Thus far we have tried to identify and evaluate the trading area. But it must be realized that the trading area is not homogeneous, and the impact of competition varies in different parts of this trading area. In other words, those who are closer to the retailing complex may frequent it more often; however, if there are other shopping complexes nearby, they would be tempted to frequent those also. But perhaps, above all, with the trading area there are multiple possibilities for a retailing site.

SINGLING OUT THE SITE

Concerning the location of a proposed retail facility, be it a single store or a complex of stores such as a shopping center, it is essential that there be multiple choices. If there is only one choice, the retailer-to-be may become too uncritical of the available location and may overlook the shortcomings of the proposed site. This kind of bias could prove to be detrimental later on.

Assuming that there are four possible sites in the general trading area under scrutiny, it is necessary to develop a checklist and analyze each site accordingly. Exhibit 5-6 is developed for that purpose. As can be seen, sixteen criteria are presented in the exhibit. Certainly the number and nature of the criteria used could vary based on unique conditions or on the preferences of the management of the proposed retailing concern. Each site is evaluated by the combined scoring of the sixteen criteria. The scoring used here has been (1) for the best-case scenario and (10) for the worst-case scenario. It is clear that Site 1 is by far the best. It must be added, however, that in our evaluation we have given equal weight to all sixteen variables. In certain circum-

Exhibit 5-6. Site Evaluation Checklist

FEATURES	SITE 1	SITE 2	SITE 3	SITE 4
Traffic congestion (vehicular)	1	4	6	8
Highways connecting to the site	4	3	8	5
Adequacy of exits	1	2	3	2
Adequacy of parking	1	5	4	8
Attractiveness to pedestrians	4	4	8	6
Pedestrian safety	4	6	7	5
Density of pedestrian traffic	3	3	6	7
Landlords are cooperative	1	2	5	2
Maintenance of the facility	2	2	4	8
Availability of long term leases	2	2	3	7
Rents are expected to be stable	1	2	2	3
Low level of absentee ownership	1	1	1	2
Economic and business activity is promising	2	4	5	7
Competition is not overwhelming	2	4	2	7
Proximity to other supportive retailing	1	4	3	8
Residents in the area are a good target	1	3	4	3
TOTAL	**31**	**51**	**71**	**88**

stances the weights given to the variables could be different, and a weighted average total of each site would need to be calculated. Despite the sixteen specific variables identified in Exhibit 5-6, a proposed site needs to be analyzed in more general terms also. In such an analysis, traffic and history, accessibility and legal aspects must be considered.

Traffic and History

Throughout this book, it is reiterated that traffic is the lifeblood of retailing. If a site is in a mall or a shopping center, then pedestrian traffic must be explored. On the other hand, if a location is considered for a new shopping center, a cluster, or a solo-standing store, then it is necessary to analyze vehicular traffic. Along with pedestrian traffic counts, it is valuable to obtain supplemental information. Information obtained in this way can be of particular value. If, for example, we were able to discover how far consumers are likely to go to buy home electronics, then we could determine the chances of the proposed store's success. Thus, combining traffic counts with individual surveys can be very useful.

In analyzing the history of the proposed site, it is important to know how this particular site was used previously. If, for instance, we are considering this particular site for a gas station and three similar undertakings died on the same site, we need to examine the proposed business in question more carefully. It would be inappropriate to think that the previous retailers could not make it but we can. And if the site is not adequate, success in retailing is impossible. In analyzing the site's history, it is also critical to determine what happened to other retail establishments in the immediate area so we may know what is likely to happen to us. Knowing the proximity to other stores that are complementary to our proposed retail establishment is a powerful factor for us; we must be clear what is near to the site and whether a steady relationship with the stores that are near to the site in consideration is likely to remain. International Rug Imports is a case in question. The store had a very good selection of Turkish and Persian rugs at very good prices. It was located at a high-traffic corner of a regional shopping center. However, its location was between a drug store and a supermarket. People who are likely to buy expensive imported rugs are not likely to do their grocery shopping or go to drug stores in the same trip. International Rug Imports went out of business in less than six months.

Accessibility

If a site is evaluated on the basis of its proximity alone, that may prove to be a costly error. Even though a site might be considered in good proximity, it may have excessive traffic congestion. Therefore, during certain times of the day it may not be very accessible. If vehicular traffic is being analyzed for the site in question, at least five issues need to be clarified:

1. Is the site capable of generating customer traffic?
2. What are the specific features that would enhance the attractiveness of our planned retail facility?
3. How safe is the area for pedestrians?
4. What is the expected growth potential of the pedestrian traffic?
5. What is the growth potential in the immediate trading area?

These are very general questions. Each would lead to numerous additional questions that are specific and important for our retail venture. However, most of these are actual types of retailing specifics that need to be examined carefully as an area is being evaluated.

Legal Aspects

Every potential and actual site has certain legal dimensions that need to be examined. Samli (1998) identified five of these. These are zoning laws, landlord responsibilities, renter responsiveness, rent values, and land ownership.

How changeable the zoning laws are is the first critical question. If they are very changeable and we cannot plan how to cope with future competition, future taxes, and future growth, we may have to stay away from a particular site. Similarly, zoning laws may change in such a way that they may enhance or hinder economic development. This could be rather dangerous.

Since most retailers are more likely to lease than build, responsibilities of the landlords in regard to maintaining the area, the facilities, and the specific building is critical. If the landlords are not committed to upkeep—maintaining and improving buildings and grounds—then the retailer needs to stay away. Furthermore, if the management or the property owners are unrealistic in their demands about rent, maintenance, and other related areas, these matters could be very damaging to the prospective retailer.

Renter responsibilities need to be arrived at jointly rather than dictated by the landlord groups. Of course, the other renters' behavior can be critical for a prospective retailer. If, for instance, it is detected that other renters are not fulfilling their responsibility of maintaining the physical facilities and surroundings and are considering leaving the premises, the proposed retail facility should be very hesitant to locate there.

Rent values can be and/or can become very unrealistic. In many cases when the properties are owned by absentee owners or property owners are leaving the area, they may charge exorbitant rental rates. Similarly, some property owners may tie the rents to the national price index, which may be too high for the particular community in question. The prospective retailer, in addition to being sensitive to these issues, must also be able to judge a reasonable rental rate by evaluating the strengths and weaknesses of a proposed site.

Finally, land and property ownership can create a major legal problem. For instance, if the owner dies and multiple heirs cannot agree on certain terms, the prospective retailer may find herself in a very difficult situation.

ASSESSING MARKET POTENTIAL

Once the site is singled out, it is critical to assess what that site could generate in terms of sales volume. Earlier in this chapter we explored how much sales volume may be generated in the area under study, but all things being the same, the share of that volume for the proposed retail facility is the key question. Regarding the retail facility being planned, at least two approaches become critical: first, establishing an average size for the establishment, and, second, measuring store saturation level. Average establishment size would depend upon dollar sales per square foot for each trade line, estimated total trade, and number of establishments in the area. The following formula could help conceptualize this issue:

$$\text{Average Establishment Size} = \frac{\textit{Estimated Total Trade}}{\textit{Dollar sales per sq. foot} \cdot \textit{Number of Stores}}$$

Given the average size for a proposed retail facility, if we plan more than, say, doubling that, we face a serious risk of not being able to sell enough.

Along with the average establishment size, store saturation level is also critical. The store saturation level indicates whether there are more than the necessary number of stores in the area and what the trend may be in this direction. Here is considered the number of customers and how much they spend on the line of merchandise in question and the number of stores dealing with that product line. The following can be used for store saturation evaluation.

$$\text{Store Saturation Level} = \frac{\textit{Number of Customers} \cdot \textit{Average Expenditures}}{\textit{Number of Retail Establishments}}$$

Assuming there is an idea of how much the store might sell to break even in general terms, if the analysis presented above shows a larger sum, this could be very attractive. However, if further analysis indicates that, while the area population is stable, the number of retail establishments is increasing, then it may be concluded that the site in question is not as attractive as it appeared to be at first sight.

One additional method of evaluation of the site calls for establishing the total sales in the area, as presented in Exhibits 5-2 and 5-3, then approximating the square footage of the area by simply walking through the establishments that trade the product line in question, say, groceries, apparel, or toys. Knowing what the national averages are for these products in terms of sales per square foot, we can establish if the proposed site has above or below average figures. If it is above average, that means the area is already overcrowded. If it is below average, there is likely potential for selling.

ESTIMATING SALES POTENTIAL
FOR THE PROPOSED STORE

Once the area potential is established, then it becomes necessary to determine how much of this total can be the proposed store's sales volume. Here additional information relating to (1) demographics and income levels, and (2) purchasing behavior and spending patterns of the people in the area needs to be examined.

Exhibit 5-7 illustrates an estimate of sales potential for the proposed store. Let us assume that the proposed retail establishment is an apparel store and, conservatively, about 10 percent of annual income goes to apparel. Of that 10 percent, the proposed store is likely to capture about 30 percent, since there are only

Exhibit 5-7. Site Evaluation Checklist

Number of households in the retail trading area	1,500 households
	X
Average annual income of the households in the trading area	50,000
	X
How much of this income goes into purchasing the products sold by the store	0.10
	X
The estimated proportion of money spent on the product line that will be spent in the proposed store	0.30
	X
The proportion of this total that will go to competing stores (−)	0.10
	=
Sales potential of the proposed store (approximate rounded)	$2,400,000 per year

two other stores in the area. But a safety measure of an additional 10 percent is allocated for these stores. If the estimates are reasonable and the retail establishment performs well, the annual gross sales are expected to be around $2,400,000.

CAPITAL NEEDS ESTIMATION

Once we establish that the proposed store could make around $2,400,000, it is critical to determine the capital needs of this project to get started. Our discussion so far has been only a means to an end. Without establishing the store's capital needs, there could not be a true assessment of this store's feasibility.

When small businesses fail, often the excuse given is that the enterprise was undercapitalized. Unless there are adequate funds, a business should not get started. However, it is also possible that the business was not managed properly and, therefore, ran out of capital. Exhibit 5-8 provides some basic ballpark figures that can be used to establish the capital needs. First, let us assume that 60 percent of sales is cost of goods sold. It is reasonable to assume a revolving credit of six months. Hypothetically we assume that the inventory turnover rate, which indicates how many times the average inventory is sold in the course of a year, is about three. Based on these inputs and the data in Exhibit 5-7, the following calculations take place. Sixty percent of $2,400,000

Exhibit 5-8. Operating Expenditures in Percentages*

Net Sales	100.0
Cost of Goods Sold	60.0
Cost of Operations	23.8
Rent	2.9
Interest	0.7
Depreciation	0.8
Pensions	0.3
Other (Promotion)	14.4
Compensation	3.0
Taxes	1.3
Projected Profit Margin after Taxes	3.3

Source: Adapted and revised from Samli, 1998.

*These types of figures are available at U.S. Department of Commerce Offices of Small Business Administration

is $1,440,000. This number, divided by three, would yield approximately $480,000. Since there is a six-month revolving credit, and inventory turnover rate is three, $480,000 is divided by six. This would yield $80,000. This is what would be needed for two months of inventory.

It is also critical to realize that for about the first two months of operation, the store will not yield any profit. These two months must be covered. Forty percent of $2,400,000 is about $960,000, and two months equivalent is $160,000. This amount is two months' cost of operations. Although in Exhibit 5-8 the cost of operations is shown to be 23.8 percent, 40 percent was taken as a precautionary measure at the beginning. This brings the capital requirements to $240,000 (160,000 + 80,000). In addition to operating costs for two months, there are preopening expenditures. These expenditures are not excessive, since the land and buildings are included in the rent. The site is likely to be made operational for the retailer by the landlord. However, there are some expenditures, such as store layout, display windows, signs, promotionals, and other expenditures. Anywhere between 10 and 25 percent of the monthly revenues may be allocated for about two months. The monthly revenue is averaged around $200,000 ($2,400,000 12 = $180,000). Ten percent of $360,000 (two month's revenue) is $36,000, which will be added to total capital requirements. Added on to $240,000, the total capital requirements reach $276,000. It must be reiterated that pre-opening promotional activity is one of the most serious expense items. It is covered in the cost of operations, but is also supplemented by the $36,000 additional funding up front.

Taking an industry average of profits for small and medium-sized stores, 3.3 percent after taxes, yields about $79,000. If the capital requirements are about $276,000 and net profit is $79,000, then about 29 percent return ($79,000 $276,000) is calculated. All things being the same, this is a good return for investment, and the project can be looked upon favorably. This store appears to be quite an attractive investment proposition. It must be further reiterated, however, that allowing 40 percent rather than 23.8 percent (Exhibit 5-8) for expenses for the first two months provides a safety cushion. It is also reasonable to expect no profit at the beginning. Thus, our capitalization estimates made provision for that contingency.

SUMMARY

Without proper location decisions, a retailer cannot survive. It is therefore critical that major research activity go into this phase of analysis. Seven steps are discussed in conjunction with this analysis. These are the following: (1) identify the particular area; (2) delimit the trading area; (3) single out the site; (4) assess market potentials; (5) estimate sales potential; (6) estimate capital needs; (7) decide whether to go or not.

Within these seven steps there are many activities. Two points need to be particularly reinforced: First, there is much that can be done in this all-important area; therefore, additional creativity and effort will go a long way. Second, without careful analysis of capital needs and a reasonable approximation of return on investment, a store is taking a big risk. It is not necessarily true that the procedures presented in this chapter indicate a fail-safe guaranteed approach, but they do reduce the failure risk and need to be considered very carefully.

REFERENCES

Samli, A. Coskun (1998), *Strategic Marketing for Success in Retailing*, Westport, CT: Quorum Books.

6

Consumer Behavior and Retail Strategy

The retailer's success is directly related to understanding consumer behavior, particularly the behavior of the store's customers. Here the point must be made emphatically that understanding consumer behavior is not for the purpose of exploiting consumers but to satisfy their needs better so that they will come back to the store again and again. The key to success is creation of customer value.

A CONSUMER BEHAVIOR MODEL IS THE ESSENCE

A retailer, any retailer, must understand what makes consumers behave the way they do. Although a retailer cannot change the internal workings of such behavior, a retailer can influence it by advertising and other attempts to communicate. Furthermore, retail marketing strategies can be modified to cater to customer behavior. Although there is no one retail consumer behavior model, the model presented here is very functional and facilitates retail marketing strategies accordingly.

Exhibit 6-1 presents such a model. Consumer behavior, in conjunction with retailing, has three major phases: prepurchase behavior, purchase behavior and postpurchase behavior. The first explores just how consumers (preferably our customers) decide that they need certain products or services. The second delves into how consumers (preferably our customers) choose these stores, products, and brands. The third examines the thought process that will keep customers away from our store or bring them back to our store again and again. Here, understanding cognitive dissonance (or buyer remorse) is critical so that it can be avoided.

Consumer behavior, as a discipline, has enjoyed great success during the past four decades or so. Many models, explaining

Exhibit 6-1. Consumer Behaviors as They Apply to Retailing

```
┌──────────────┐      ┌──────────────────┐      ┌──────────────┐
│   Cultural   │◄─────│ Need Realization │◄─────│  Individual  │
│  Background  │      │Shopping Motivation│      │ Personality  │
└──────────────┘      └──────────────────┘      └──────────────┘
        │                      │                        ▲
        ▼                      ▼                        │
 Prepurchase          ┌──────────────────┐              │
 Behavior,            │Shopper Characteristics│         │
 Consumer            │and Shopping Behavior│           │
        │             └──────────────────┘      Retail Follow-
        │                      │                 up Strategy
        ▼                      ▼
 Prepurchase         ┌──────────────────────┐
 Behavior,           │Identifying Retail Consumer│
 Retailer            │  Behavior Patterns   │
        │            └──────────────────────┘
        │              │        │        │
        ▼              ▼        ▼        ▼
 Purchase      ┌───────┐ ┌───────┐ ┌───────┐
 Behavior      │ Store │ │ Brand │ │Product│
               │Choice │◄►│Choice │◄►│Choice │
               │Behavior│ │Behavior│ │Behavior│
               └───────┘ └───────┘ └───────┘
                   │        │        │
                   ▼        ▼        ▼
               ┌──────────────────────┐
 Postpurchase  │ Degree of Satisfaction│
 Behavior      │    Store Loyalty     │
               │    Buyer Remorse     │
               │ Cognitive Dissonance │
               └──────────────────────┘
```

Source: Adapted and Revised from Samli, 1998.

some of the most intimate aspects of this behavior, have surfaced and are discussed, tested, and incorporated into our general marketing knowledge base. Unfortunately, however, only a very small proportion of this research effort and knowledge base has been allocated to retailing. Thus, retailing still suffers from not receiving its fair share from our ever-increasing knowledge of consumer behavior (Samli 1998).

It is, therefore, clear that any attempt to understand and explain this very complex retail consumer behavior, that is multiphased and influenced by multiple factors, is invaluable. This is how retailers can be of greater service to their customers and generate greater consumer value. A critical point must be made regarding Exhibit 6-1. The prepurchase behavior needs to be explored from the consumer point of view as well as the retailer point of view. If the retailer understands shopper characteristics and shopping behavior, he or she can identify retail consumer behavior patterns accordingly.

CULTURE, PERSONALITY AND SHOPPING BEHAVIOR

The consumer behavior model presented in Exhibit 6-1 begins on one end with cultural background and ends with individual personality. Culture, according to many thinkers and researchers, is the basic force behind consumer behavior. It has been maintained that an individual is influenced by a culture screen, which develops the personality and behavior pattern (Samli 1995). Stated differently, all people are products of a culture and, as such, they behave, in broad terms, the way that culture dictates.

Based on this assertion, cultural background and personality must be considered simultaneously, and behavioral patterns must be analyzed accordingly. In the United States there are many minorities, such as Asian-Americans, Hispanic-Americans and African-Americans. Additionally, there are subcultures among the majority, mainly based on economic diversities. Though there have been many attempts to classify cultures or subcultures in conjunction with retailing, mass cultural dichotomies and their impact on retail purchase behavior have not been quite as readily recognizable. Here we dichotomize consumer behavior between individualistic and collectivistic subcultures (Samli 1995).

Exhibit 6-2 examines these two dichotomous cultures as they relate to retailing.Consumers in an individualistic culture are more self-reliant. They are primarily influenced by cognitive influences (facts, direct learning, and information). Although at the periphery they are also influenced by social class and a hierarchy of needs that influences the realization of perceived needs, at the core the purchase process is initiated by the individual himself or herself. This is why self-service has been so critical in major shopping complexes throughout the United States. Affective influences (beliefs and values) play a less critical role than cognitive influences (information and knowledge gathered by the individual) in retail purchase behavior. Studies have shown, for

Exhibit 6-2. Cultural Differences and Retail Shopping

INDIVIDUALISTIC CONSUMER	COLLECTIVISTIC CONSUMER
• Influenced primarily by cognitive forces. Makes up his/her mind based on the information collected	• Influenced by the group and its values. Affective influences and group pressures are more prominent.
• Has the initiative to search for goods and services until they are found.	• Economic necessities and preferences articulated by the group are critical.
• Influenced more by hierarchy of needs and social class than the group to which he/she belongs.	• Certain opinion leaders or family elders usually decide what is to be purchased and details regarding how, what, where, when, etc.
• Sensitive to information regarding the store, product, and brand.	• Sensitive to opinions and values by the group or opinion leaders regarding store, product, and brand.
• Not typically loyal to store, brand, or product.	• More store, brand, and product loyal.
• In store uses own initiative and search process.	• In store often follows storekeepers' directions.

Source: Adapted and revised from Samli, 1998.

example, that while white American professional women rely on their own judgment, African-American counterparts rely more heavily on suggestions of store personnel. The same behavior patterns are observed in the behavior of Asian-Americans. Particularly the first generation of this group shop in ethnic retail stores and are very close to store personnel, whereas the second generation show relatively less ethnicity. As was mentioned earlier in the Introduction, since minority populations are growing more than proportionately, such observations will enhance the success probabilities of small-scale retailers by emphasizing ethnicity and personalized service.

On the other hand, other individuals such as extended family elders or other opinion leaders influence consumers in collectivistic subcultures. They more often learn from others based on affective influences. Economic necessities play a critical role in their behavior patterns and values. Certain beliefs and values (affective influences) are instilled in individuals by others in their immediate circles (Samli 1995). These influences have very significant retailing implications. Most minorities in the United States display many aspects of this type of consumer behavior, with some minor variations perhaps because they are more cohesive and interdependent.

In these two different cultures, consumer behavior regarding retailing is significantly different; therefore, retailers must develop certain practices to cater to these differing behaviors and resultant needs.

The two separate cultures, as indicated in Exhibit 6-2, display differences in their retail shopping behavior, and these differences lead to clear-cut retail practices. The six key points of difference depicted in the exhibit should lead to the following retail practices:

First, in addressing individualistic consumer behavior there will be more emphasis on advertising directly to the individual consumer. It is quite likely that more e-tail advertising will be used in this respect as well. The collectivistic consumer, on the other hand, will be reached through advertising to the opinion leaders and family elders.

The individualistic consumer will exercise more initiative to search for products and stores than the collectivistic consumer. The latter will be influenced, again, by others. They will choose stores that are recommended to them by opinion leaders and family elders.

Individualistic consumers, of course, also have values and are influenced by social class differences and the hierarchy of needs. But, in general, they rely on information they gather on their own. Collectivistic consumers get their values more readily from the groups that they are involved in.

If individualistic consumers are making decisions according to their need perception, then they are likely to be more sensitive to information about products, stores, and brands. But the collectivistic consumers are either making decisions for others or under the influence of others.

Store loyalty of individualistic consumers can easily be questioned, since they may go by newly received information. Collectivistic consumers are more likely to be loyal to store, brand, and product.

Finally, individualistic consumers are *activity oriented.* They prefer to explore on their own in self-service stores. They prefer to do their own exploration and gather their own information, whereas collectivistic consumers are *attribute oriented.* They prefer to talk to storekeepers, salespeople,and others about the store, product, and brand features, especially in department stores and boutiques. They go by the impressions given to them by opinion leaders, family elders, or storekeepers.

As can be seen, these features and pronounced differences can easily guide retailers in their retail marketing activities. More is discussed regarding these points throughout this book.

CONTRASTS IN IN-STORE BEHAVIOR

The dichotomy of attribute orientation versus activity orientation leads to noticeable contrasts between the in-store behavior of two culturally different consumer groups. Exhibit 6-3 displays some of the key contrasts between the two.

Attribute orientation, which is tied into collectivistic consumer behavior, pays attention to the detail about store features and the salespeople who are reinforcing these features. Collectivistic consumers ask store attendants and salespeople for advice and direction. The individualistic consumer, on the other hand, adapts activity orientation which focuses on the individual's own efforts to shop around and find things in the store. More focus on self-service, along with more self-effort to accumulate

Exhibit 6-3. In-Store Shopper Behavior

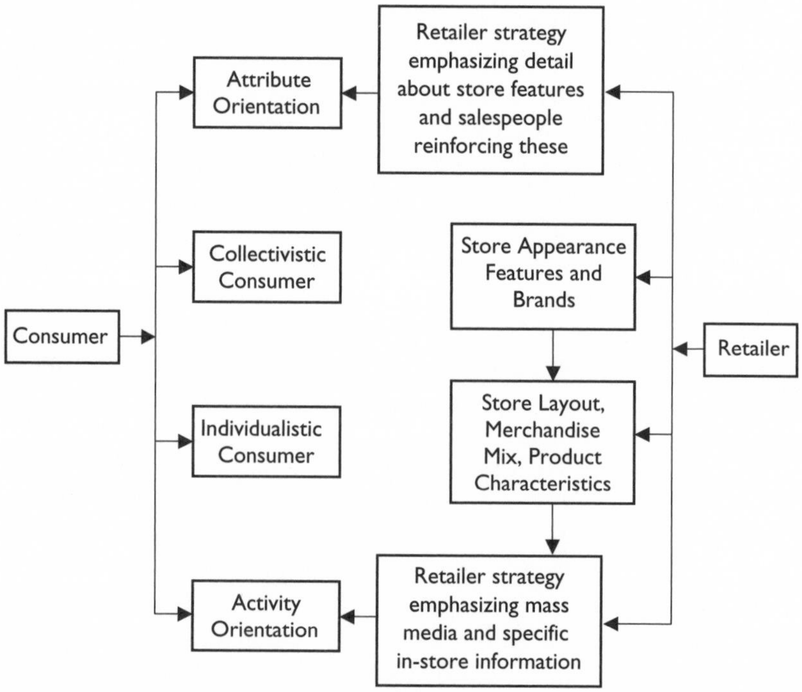

information about the store, merchandise, and brands, makes this behavior different from the attribute orientation of the collectivistic consumer. The retailer's strategy in these two extreme situations has to be catering primarily to the group that is the store's target market. A store's appearance and features, along with the personnel, are to be considered carefully and prepared for both the attribute or activity orientation. Similarly, in-store logistics, which deals with the merchandise mix displayed and where it is displayed in the store, needs to accommodate these two orientations. Finally, the information flow out of the store or promotional efforts of the retail establishment need to be adjusted, depending upon whether the primary concern is collectivistic consumer behavior or individualistic consumer behavior. The collectivistic consumer collects information from others, and the individualistic consumer collects her own information.

Even though these two cultural camps have different reasons and approaches to patronizing retail stores, in general terms they still have certain basic shopping motives. Although these motives are somewhat similar, they surface in different forms for the two cultural groups or subcultures.

SHOPPING MOTIVES AND RETAIL PRACTICES

Every retailer should realize that not all consumers patronize a retail facility for the same reason. In fact, people frequent retail facilities for different reasons. Retailers must realize just why people shop and, more importantly, why they shop in the retail facility where they shop.

Need realization and shopping motivation are presented in Exhibit 6-1 as the first consideration. Just how people realize that they do need certain products or services and what it would take for consumers to be motivated to go to certain retail establishments to shop are extremely critical issues.

A few attempts have been made to determine the shopping motives that consumers experience (Samli 1998). Ten motives have been identified as the most important factors behind retail shopping. These are:

1. *Diversion*—consumers need to get away to break away from dullness of daily routines.
2. *Self-gratification*—a special stimulation of the individual's psyche is created by the shopping process within a certain ambience.

3. *Learning about new trends or fashions*—since there are new products and services that are entering the retail sector along with new fashions, individuals can learn much about them as they shop around.

4. *Physical activity*—walking around in large shopping complexes may be the only exercise and relaxation some people may receive in their hectic lives.

5. *Sensory stimulation*—by seeing, touching, smelling or trying on the products, individuals can experience sensory satisfaction.

6. *Social experiences outside the home*—socializing with friends and other customers, going to shop with friends, and interacting with store personnel all provide special motivation.

7. *Pleasure of negotiation and choice selection*—being able to compare, contrast, and negotiate the terms of the purchase in order to find best buys is a critical stimulator.

8. *Satisfying clearly identified needs and wants*—effort made to satisfy needs by shopping is a critical foundation of retailing.

9. *Peer pressures or opinion leader influences*—individuals are influenced by others to buy certain things to be part of new trends.

10. *To satisfy shopping needs efficiently*—being able to shop efficiently is an important motivator.

As is specified in Exhibit 6-1, prepurchase behavior begins with shopping motivation. The ten shopping motives discussed here are also presented in Exhibit 6-4. In the exhibit, the retail practices that are appropriate for each shopping motive are further specified. Implementing retail strategies with such practical activities give a special advantage to the individual retailer. However, the retail practices section of Exhibit 6-4 must be carefully understood and implemented. These practices differentiate the stores and create differential congruence for a retail establishment. Each retail establishment must consider which of the ten shopping motives are most appropriate for its particular clientele and then must decide how its retail practices must be implemented in order to cater to these shopping motives.

Although, in a general sense, any one of the ten motives discussed here may not play a more critical role in the consumer's shopping behavior than any other, in the case of specific shopper groups or market segments, the situation may be completely reversed. Some of these motives in specific market segments may play a substantially more important role than others. Of course it is rather obvious that these ten motives are not totally mutually

Exhibit 6-4. Shopping Motives vs. Retail Practices

INDIVIDUALISTIC CONSUMER	COLLECTIVISTIC CONSUMER
1. Diversion from daily routine	Making the store visit exciting
2. Self-gratification	Helping consumers to make good purchase decisions by giving choice and information
3. Learning about new trends or fashions	Carrying most up-to-date products with good information
4. Physical activity	Customers can walk around freely and safely as they try out products
5. Sensory stimulation	Attractive arrangements and appearances, and allowing consumers to feel, try on, or try out products
6. Social experiences outside the home	Having an opportunity to socialize in the store with the personnel and other customers
7. Pleasure of negotiation and choice selection	Giving an opportunity to negotiate, analyze, compare products, and discuss them with others
8. Satisfying clearly identified needs and wants	Making sure that the store is known to carry certain products all the time; helping customers to shop quickly
9. Peer pressures or opinion leader influences	The store carries certain products that are subject to influences such as new models, new fashions, etc.
10. To satisfy shopping needs efficiently	Proper pre-purchase communication, adequate emphasis on e-trade, in-store adjustments such as express lanes, etc.

exclusive, in that they may interact with one another. Having analyzed these ten shopping motives leads to the conclusion that there are multiple shopping behaviors. It is very critical that retailers understand shopper characteristics that are triggered by the ten shopping motives. Without such an understanding, it would be very difficult for retailers to delight their customers, which is the ultimate goal.

GROUPING SHOPPERS

Exhibit 6-5 illustrates an attempt to group shoppers and connect them to the shopping motives presented in Exhibit 6-4. Although the classification of the groups and their shopping motives is

Exhibit 6-5. Shopper Groupings

	SHOPPER DESCRIPTION	PURCHASE MOTIVATION
Agreeable Shoppers 23%	Lower-middle income, shopping at discount stores, much mass media exposure. Brand loyal for everything.	Clearly identified needs and wants, specific pressures.
Practical Shoppers 22%	Research purchases in advance, looking for best deals, middle income, younger, better educated, women. Buy modern frills. Not too brand loyal.	Pleasure of bargaining, learning about new trends. Extensive Internet search.
Trendy Shoppers 17%	Impulse buyers. Prefer latest fads. Frequent fashion boutiques. Mostly young. Not much brand loyalty. Need many products. Prefer imports.	Self-gratification, sensory stimulation.
Value Shoppers 15%	Cost conscious. Brand loyal. Prefer old, accepted products and brands. Frequent department stores. Older, higher than average income. Consider shopping a chore.	Clearly identified needs. Satisfying shopping needs efficiently.
Top-of-the-line Shoppers 10%	Shop at upscale department stores. Equate quality with reputation. Older, highest median income. Prefer imports.	Social experiences, diversion, self-gratification.
Safe Shoppers 9%	Prefer familiarity. Tradition. Do not like shopping. Go to well-known mass merchandisers.	Clearly identified needs. Specific pressures to shop.
Status Shoppers 5%	Impractical. Like new gadgets. Second highest median income. Spend much time on shopping, but also buy on impulse.	Physical activity, social experiences, self-gratification, learning about new trends, satisfying shopping needs efficiently.

Source: Adapted and revised from Samli, 1998.

somewhat arbitrary, it is maintained here that any retailer that can look at the store's clientele and group them, connect them to certain shopping motives, and identify the retail practices that can be effectively used for these groups is bound to be successful. It takes objective understanding and caring for customers to be successful in retailing. Each retailer may find variations, additions, and deletions in the classification presented in Exhibit 6-5. Although the sum total percentages add up to 100 percent, a typical retailer may be working with only one or two of these seven categories. A special comment about e-trade is in order here. In recent years, there has been an increase in e-trading. Certainly this is likely to increase. However, just who buys through the

Internet and why needs to be identified and connected to other aspects of purchase motivation. Of the seven groups described in Exhibit 6-5, safe shoppers are the most likely group to use the Internet for their shopping needs. This is because they do not like the physical activity attached to shopping. This does not mean that cyberspace cannot be used for contacting other groups. It simply means that this group is most likely to be active in this area.

It is strongly suggested that individual and proactive retailers generate their own information about grouping customers and identifying their purchase motives related to need perception, store selection, product preferences, brand recognition, and other factors influencing shopping behavior. Modern retailers must always be on the lookout for additional information that will enable them to satisfy their customers and encourage them to come back.

Needless to say, prepurchase activities, postpurchase activities, and behavior patterns (Exhibit 6-1) are extremely critical for the retailer's survival. Although these three major phases of shopper behavior may differ from one retail complex to another, understanding these and manipulating them is the key to differential congruence and retail success.

THE PURCHASE PROCESS

Need realization on the part of the prospective consumer begins with perception. The consumer is constantly exposed to mass media and other types of information and promotion. Each individual is different; therefore, the messages and information received are interpreted somewhat differently. As the individual decodes these messages and information, a purchase need recognition surfaces. This need recognition is further interpreted by the individual in terms of a product or service, a brand, and a store. This interpretation by the individual indicates a powerful job by retail marketing. The enhancement of the purchase need can take place both at the conscious and subconscious levels. When a consumer receives a stimulus that is related to shopping, it is received at a threshold from which it may penetrate the conscious or subconscious levels. At the subconscious level, the stimulus may establish an image of the product, brand, or store. At the conscious level, however, it may enhance the image of the product, brand, or store, or all three. The subconscious appeal, if intentionally attempted, as in the case of subliminal advertising, is not legal and is likely to take effect in the longer run. Thus, the retailer will do better by attempting to penetrate the conscious level with faster and more tangible results. However, it may be maintained that any message or stimulus would have, at least nominally, a subconscious appeal. That could accumulate and make the retailer's short-run efforts much more effective by creating a synergistic impact. A consumer's buying behavior starts with a stimulus perception. As the perception brings about a problem recognition, the consumer begins acquiring some information or receiving certain messages that are related to the recognized problem. Since consumer information is critical for the retailer, the retailer must understand the consumer's information search process.

Information regarding retail shopping comes from different sources. Those who have lived in an area longer may get more information from friends and relatives than those who are new in the area. The latter may receive more information from the mass media. Here an important theory comes into play. This is named "Weber's Law." It states that as the stimulus intensities get stronger, it will take more of a change in a new stimulus to be noticed. In other words, for a stimulus to become important, it must have a "just noticeable difference" that must be somewhat more of an attention-getter than other stimuli (Wilkie 1994). Every retailer must explore attention-getting activities that will make a difference.

As the problem is recognized by the prospective consumer that there is a need or desire for a service or a product, this recognition may have different degrees of intensity. The more successful the retail marketing strategy is, the greater is the recognized problem's intensity. If the retailer is capable of solving important consumer problems, it implies that there is a successful retailing strategy at work. Obviously the problem needs to be intense enough so that the consumer feels the need to buy the product or service in question. The greater the intensity of the recognized problem, the greater are the probabilities for the brand image and store image to become critical reinforcers of that intensity and therefore influence the consumer to frequent the store. Of course, some or all of the shopping motives discussed earlier also come into play, meaning that the retailer must keep all of the shopping motives in mind all the time.

As the stimuli are perceived and the problem is recognized, consumers begin an information search. All buyers search for some information. This search could be conscious or unconscious. But, since consumer shopping behavior is learned, shoppers must have a basic learning process that is stimulated by conscious consumer information search. Shopping for groceries at, say, Publix or buying home repair supplies at Home Depot or buying shoes at Payless Shoe Source all call for basic learning processes that lead in the direction of store loyalties. However, as discussed in Exhibit 6-2, the differences in cultural backgrounds lead individualistic consumers to search and receive information differently from collectivistic consumers.

The consumer search process is composed of two separate search activities, internally triggered and externally triggered. But these two separate search activities also take place in two separate arenas: in-store and out-of-store. Internally triggered search activity by individualistic consumers may lead first in the direction of store-generated information. This may lead to more cognitive influences by mass media, leading to an external search.

On the other hand, collectivistic consumers are motivated by external affective influences which are further reinforced by store employees or salespeople's influences (interpersonal), which leads to some internal search. But collectivistic consumers are more influenced by those who have had some external search for information. All these influences are affective, influenced by others, rather than cognitive, or self-learned.

In the final analysis, the information search leads in the direction of store or brand selection. Here, regardless of which one, store or brand, plays a more critical role, if they are congruent, that is, if the store is not too good to carry a very cheap brand or vice versa, then the whole process leads to a purchase activity.

As indicated in Exhibit 6-1, however, the retail consumer shopping process does not end at the point of purchase. The retailer must understand postpurchase behavior if customers are expected to come back again and again.

POSTPURCHASE ACTIVITIES

Retailing does not stop at the point where the purchase transaction is completed. Peters (1989) stated that it is five times more costly to get new customers than to keep current customers happy so that they repeat purchases. Festinger (1957) generated the theory of *cognitive dissonance.* This theory relates to what is called, in common parlance, "buyer's remorse." If, for whatever reason, a customer develops second thoughts about a recent purchase and does not feel very good about shopping in a specific store and/or about the merchandise that was purchased, then there is cognitive dissonance, and the consumer is not likely to come back.

If a retailer cannot eliminate such postpurchase blues, then that particular establishment is in deep trouble. The problem may be generated by pressure-selling tactics, less-than-adequate customer services, questionable quality merchandise, but perhaps above all, by a lack of follow-up. To counter cognitive dissonance, the retailer must find out just what caused the problem and eliminate it immediately.

The retail store must conduct postpurchase efforts—in store cards, phone calls, mail surveys, e-mail, or out–of-store follow-up—to find out how satisfied their customers are, if they are planning to come back, and if they would recommend the store to others. Similarly, stores must be sensitive to customer complaints It is possible to determine if there is customer attrition based on postpurchase dissatisfaction. The retailer must be able to determine the extent of postpurchase attrition and stop it quickly. Contacting the customer after purchase, exercising liberal return policies, and reemphasizing customer-recourse practices of the store all counter buyer's remorse.

IMPLICATIONS FOR SEGMENTATION

Nobody more than a retailer in the market system can appreciate the fact that markets are not homogeneous. A retailer, as seen in this chapter, deals with submarkets, which are market segments, that are identified as shopper groups, and each one of these shopper groups is influenced by one or more purchase motives that have been discussed.

However, an attempt to identify the target markets that a retailer deals with as agreeable, practical,and the like, is inadequate because this classification is not tangible enough. In addition to attitudes or behavior patterns, market segments need to be identified on the basis of demographics and other observable and tangible common characteristics. Exhibit 6-6 presents basic criteria for retail segmentation. Perhaps the most important message the exhibit relays is that not only are there many ways of identifying and interacting with market segments, it is almost impossible to cater to all. Even Wal-Mart, the largest retailer in

Exhibit 6-6. Basic Criteria for Retail Segmentation

CRITERIA	EXAMPLES IN RETAIL PRACTICE
Ethnic or Cultural	
Ethnic groups	Spanish speaking shopping facilities
Certain subcultures	An overall Asian shopping complex
Demographics	
Income	High-income market vs. low-income market
Age	Elderly market, children's market
Education and occupation	Highly educated sophisticates
Sex	Male or female consumers
Sociological	
Social groups	Yuppies, WASPs, Generation X
Racial differences	African-Americans, Asian-Americans
Behavioral Measures	
Lifestyles	Jet-setters
Life cycles	Empty-nesters, young married couples
Attitudes	People who collect, people who like gadgetry
Store Loyalty	
Heavy users of certain products	Those who buy certain products more often
Regulars	Those who come to store regularly
Loyals	Those who insist on buying from the same place
Benefit	
Benefits sought	Expected satisfaction by patronizing that store
Direct benefits received	Satisfaction from the store or the product directly
Indirect benefits received	Satisfaction delayed as in gifts or health foods
Greater vs. lesser benefits	Those who have improved health from a health spa
Geography	
Distances	Those who live nearby vs. those who travel a distance
Reputation of the location	Fashionable areas of town
Inshopper vs. outshopper	The area's ability to attract from neighboring communities

Source: Adapted and revised from Samli, 1998.

the world at the writing of this book, does not bring in or appeal to the market segment that frequents Neiman Marcus or Bergdorf-Goodman. At the same time, it is rather dangerous for a retailer to focus on one market segment alone. Even a more specialized retailer, such as a chocolatier or a gift shop, is likely to appeal to multiple market segments. Therefore, it is reasonable that a retail store target more than one segment. Sometimes these segments are rather small and readily identifiable. These small markets are *niches*. A retailer that is catering to a specific niche can be rather profitable. It must be reiterated that markets are not homogeneous, and it is critical that the retail establishment identify its target market and treat it just right. It is extremely critical not only to understand the importance of segmentation, but also to develop a workable and effective segmentation process.

RETAIL SEGMENTATION PROCESS

Although most of the material presented in this chapter is applicable to retail segmentation, there is a logical sequence that the retailer must follow. At the beginning of the chapter, a retail consumer behavior model is presented. Based on the premise of a detectable consumer behavior pattern, consumers are grouped. This attempt to group consumers identified the retailing tools that can be used for these groups. Next, an analysis is presented to identify just what motivates the consumer to engage in retail activity. These three steps become particularly actionable when segmentation criteria are introduced.

For instance, if Asian-American shoppers, motivated by clearly identified needs and specified pressures by others, are frequenting the store more often than other identifiable groups, then the store may resort to ethnic or cultural segmentation. More of this group will likely frequent the store if proper appeal is employed to attract this target market. Thus, from consumer behavior to segmentation, much analysis must take place. But the end result is greater consumer value, which translates into profits. In other words, differential congruence is achieved, and both parties are happy.

SUMMARY

Retailing deals with consumer behavior. Understanding this behavior is a must. Proactive retail strategies can easily work with consumer behaviors, leading to customer satisfaction and retailing profits.

Consumer behavior in retailing is first related to cultural background. In this chapter, collectivistic versus individualistic consumer behaviors are distinguished. These are culture driven and lead to different retail strategies. Over and beyond the cultural background, retail purchase behaviors have prepurchase and postpurchase phases. In each phase the retailer must be cognizant of the fact that much proactive retail strategic behavior is required of the retailer for customers to be happy enough to return and recommend the store to friends.

In responding to consumer behavior effectively, the retailer must understand that there are ten clearly identifiable shopping motives. Each motive is dealt with in certain specific retail practices.

This chapter also deals with a very important topic, segmentation. Analyzing consumer behavior leads in the direction of segmenting the market. Different criteria are used for retail segmentation. The retailer must be in a position to decide which of these criteria are most useful for their needs.

Finally, each retailer must understand that there are shopper groups, and each group may be influenced by certain purchase motives. Keeping current customers happy is five times less costly than trying to get new customers.

REFERENCES

Festinger, Leon (1957), *A Theory of Cognitive Dissonance*, Stanford, CT: Stanford University Press.

Peters, Tom (1989), *Thriving on Chaos*, New York: Alfred A. Knopf.

Samli, A. Coskun (1995), *International Consumer Behavior*, Westport, CT: Quorum Books.

Samli, A. Coskun (1998), *Strategic Marketing for Success in Retailing*, Westport, CT: Quorum Books.

Wilkie, William L. (1994), *Consumer Behavior*, New York: John Wiley and Sons.

Strategy Alternatives

Having a game plan, a *strategy*, implies being proactive and catering to the particular target market in the most favorable manner. That means providing goods and services in the market's terms. In doing so, the retailer can achieve competitive advantage and customer loyalty. Developing competitive advantage and gaining customer loyalty demonstrates that the retail establishment has developed differential congruence and improved its probability of success.

THE THINKING OF THE RETAIL STRATEGIST

Particularly in small-scale retailing, all owner-managers are strategists. They have to have a strategic plan to implement and reinforce their proactive orientation. The retail strategist will put together a game plan that will make the store popular, catering to the target market effectively, while differentiating the store from its competitors, all in all creating a differential congruence. Unfortunately, many owner-managers are so busy with day-to-day activities, they do not make time to strategize. In such cases, the strategy is not planned and implemented; it just happens. This leaves the store not proactive, but at best reactive and mostly inactive.

Being a strategist is not just a process that happens automatically. All small retailers must think of a strategy and how to implement it, and as such they must go beyond their day-to-day manual activities so that they can think and plan.

The strategic decision process goes through at least five stages as it is presented in Exhibit 7-1. Targeting market segments is the starting point, which was discussed in Chapter 6. At any given time the retailer must realize that there are external modifiers changing the existing targeted segments as time goes by. There are at least five such modifiers influencing market segments at the retail level.

- Demographics: A continuous shift of population to the Southeast, Southwest, and Far West, for example. Changing age distribution with great increases in the proportion of the elderly. Renewed increase in birth rates.

- New values: A growing concern about the environment. Increasing interest in green products, consumerism, women's liberation, and recycling.

- Economic realities: A noticeable decrease in the income of the middle class. Losses of well-paying jobs. An increasing degree of consumer sophistication and, as incomes don't increase fast enough, consumers demanding more for their money.

- Escalating competition: Retail competition increasing. In addition to both intra- and inter-type retail competition (Chapter 2), new developments emerging. Among these e-tailing, telemarketing, and other nonstore retailing.

- New realities: As the middle class disappears, consumer markets becoming more fragmented. One-stop shopping and discount wholesaling on the rise. Dual career couples requesting different types of retailing (Samli 1998).

These and other developments are directly influencing the retailing atmosphere. Therefore, here they are named segment modifiers.

Exhibit 7-1. Strategic Decision Process

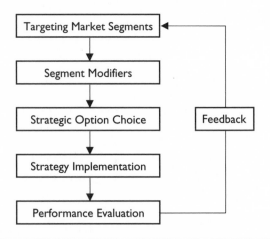

84

TYPES OF STRATEGIES

Targeting and recognizing segment modifiers help determine what strategy option to adopt and then modify as necessary. Seven strategy options are identified: general merchandising, differentiating, segmenting, positioning, niching, category killing, and guerilla fighting.

General Merchandizer

The retailer's strategy in this case is aggregating the market. This can also be named mass retailing. Typically general merchandizers start with merchandise mixes similar to those of competitors. The assumption here is that the market is large enough and that anybody can capture a portion of it by imitating others. For decades Sears, Montgomery Ward, and others thrived on convenience, variety, and ease of shopping. These retailers made a wide assortment of products available at their relatively convenient locations where one-stop shopping and scrambled merchandising took place. On a much smaller scale, many country stores located at the edge of small towns in rural America still exercise this particular strategy. This strategy emphasizes the variety, prices, events, and store location variables. Advertising, if any, dwells upon these features and is rather informative. Segmentation is not commonly exercised.

Differentiator

Although the differentiator may start with the premise that all consumers are basically alike, appeals to these consumers are made through different combinations of retail mixes. Here the strategy leads in the direction of generating a competitive edge by being different from competitors. In addition to differentiating the store with retail mixes, retailers may add such features as credit, gift wrapping, delivery, extended store hours, liberal return policy, eating facilities, fashion shows, and the like. Advertising activity dwells upon these features. All in all, the strategy is geared to creating a store image that will distinguish the store from competitors. A differentiator, however, does not think of matching the store's unique features with the target market's self-image and, hence, does not quite create a differential congruence.

Segmenter

If the retailer realizes that markets are not homogeneous, he or she starts thinking along the lines of trading areas that are composed of several homogeneous submarkets. Each of these is a segment where needs, purchase motives, and behavior patterns are quite uniform. The retailer targets one or more of these segments. Such a segmentation strategy in retailing has not been as rapid and as sophisticated as manufacturers' segmentation activity has been. However, market segmentation is becoming more and more widespread among retailers. As more small retailers enter the arena, there will be a more noticeable exercise in segmenting, which will enhance consumer value generation. The Limited, Gap, and Payless Shoes are all examples of specialty retail chains that appeal to carefully defined market segments. Particularly at the higher level, some department stores are also trying to segment. Bloomingdales, Marshall Fields and Target are obvious examples of department store chains that are involved in segmentation. Successful segmentation, by definition, generates differential congruence.

Positioner

A positioner strategist starts with orienting itself in the market place vis-à-vis specific competitors. Originally, Wal-Mart positioned itself somewhat below Sears, so that it could appeal to the fast-growing lower middle class as opposed to the somewhat shrinking upper middle class to which Sears appeals. Burger King positioned itself head-to-head with McDonald's. Wendy's positioned itself slightly above these two. One can detect such positioning strategy in almost all retailing situations. The critical point here is the deliberateness of this positioning activity. A retailer's positioning of itself without planning or even intending to do so is not quite as effective as a deliberate positioning strategy such as, for instance, Target exercises. Target stores are attempting to take some customers away from Sears and some from Wal-Mart by positioning itself between the two. This has been very successful for Target.

Nicher

A nicher starts strategizing by identifying a very carefully defined corner of the market. This corner of the market may barely have room for one retailer. The nicher assumes that it can do the best job of satisfying the needs here and profiting from catering well to this carefully defined corner of the market. In this case, by doing a good job, the retailer preempts future competition. The nicher is a very specific segmenter who is much closer to the market, from General Nutrition Centers (GNC) catering to the health and bodybuilding segments of the market, to a shoe repair store in one small community. Nichers must adjust their offerings very sharply to the needs of very well-defined corners of the market.

Category Killers

This is a very recent strategy that is still emerging. A category killer starts with the orientation that, regardless of differences in their needs, orientation, values, or buying behaviors, consumers truly go for bargains, and all people desire some product lines and many choices in each line. For instance, everyone buys a toy or two; therefore, Toys-R-Us, up to now, has been a very successful category killer. A category killer maintains better merchandise mixes with greater variety at lower prices, and believes that whatever the competitors do, it can do better, which means, primarily, cheaper. Retail chains such as Home Depot, Blockbuster Videos, and Books-A-Million are all category killers. Their successful activity, by definition, implies that they enjoy a very successful state of differential congruence. At the writing of this book a war is brewing between category killers and the new discount general merchandisers. It remains to be seen which group will win out.

Guerilla Fighter

Guerilla fighting may be considered a strategic posture that is most appropriate for small retailers. Those who have limited budgets but great will to survive are willing to do whatever it takes to survive. They fight for existence and put in a great deal of effort to satisfy their customers. What they lack in resources, variety, and credit, is compensated for by personal service and relationship marketing. These are managed hands-on, and change as conditions change. A small men's apparel shop, in time, may become a major center of uniforms, or a women's ready-to-wear clothing store may become an apparel store primarily for older women. Personal touches such as starting a fifty-plus club, sending birthday presents to members, or giving a percentage refund on all credit cards are examples of guerilla fighting strategies (Samli 1998).

Consider, for instance, the following: A caller in Florida is talking to a local florist. The caller says, "I would like to send two dozen roses to North Carolina. How much would it cost?" The store quotes a price. The caller replies, "Isn't this a bit too high?" The store's spokesperson answers, "Maybe you should call someplace else." The caller gets two other estimates. Both are about half the price the first store quoted. The customer is lost, probably for good. When we are a small establishment with no other uniqueness, it is critical that our skills in customer communications be used as guerrilla fighting tools.

Once the basic game plan (strategy) is identified, the retail establishment must plan the strategy implementation. This implementation is likely to make or break the retail establishment.

STRATEGY IMPLEMENTATION

Implementing the strategic plan is at least as important as having such a plan. Three areas of consideration are identified as most crucial in strategy implementation: retail mix combination, strategic business units (SBUs) versus profit centers, and store product combinations.

Retail Mix Combination

In Chapter 1, five retail mixes are presented as the key strategic tools in retailing. These five mixes are presented in a reasonable but not exhaustive manner. Each one of these mixes plays a different role in the implementation of the seven strategic options discussed in this chapter.

- In general terms, a general merchandising strategy calls for a special emphasis on a goods and services mix. A general merchandise selection is the crux of this strategy. But there may be a special need to cut costs some, since the store does not have many other unique features. This implies a heavy emphasis on a logistics mix also.

- In a differentiating strategy, the merchandise mix is still critical because it is different. But this difference must be communicated with the target market. Thus, the communication mix is likely to be very important.

- A segmentation strategy may call for emphasis on a special merchandise and service mix. But this basic mix may use a pricing mix as a support function along with a communication mix.

- A positioning strategy is likely to emphasize all of the mixes almost equally because it is an all-out effort to pit the store against—typically—a well-known, well-established competitor. It is a broader game plan that requires all of the mixes to come together and perform as needed.

- A niching strategy would call for heavy emphasis on a goods and service mix, along with a human resource mix. The contact with the special corner of the market must be very close; therefore, the human resource mix plays a critical role in establishing a very close interaction with customers and maintaining that level of communication throughout. A logistics mix may have a special role in in-store considerations to make the store appealing and functional.

- A category killing strategy dwells, above all, upon a pricing mix. For the same variety, the retailer is offering much better prices and more attractive deals. The cost-cutting functions to support lower prices are also critical; therefore, out-of-store logistics may be particularly critical.

- Guerilla fighting calls for heavier emphasis on the human resource mix, since many different deals may be used to conduct business. Very specialized merchandise mix and communication mixes may be used to support the variety and creativity required to survive.

It must be realized that, in retailing, each case is different and all mixes are important. This rather simplistic account of retail mixes vis-à-vis retail strategy implementation is just an attempt at consciousness-raising. A retailer must be able to plan the implementation of the strategy by considering the relative roles of retail mixes. It must be understood that all retail mixes are important, but in our unique situation, some may be more important than others. Exhibit 7-2 presents a reasonably detailed account of five retail mixes. Again, individual retailers will have to add and delete some items to make these mixes more suitable for the particular needs of the store in question.

Exhibit 7-2. Some Key Components of Retail Mixes

GOODS AND SERVICES MIX	COMMUNICATION MIX	PRICING MIX	HUMAN RESOURCE MIX	LOGISTICS MIX
Merchandise	Advertising	Price Level	Personal Selling	Out-of-Store Logistics
Variety and Assortment	Catalogs	Price Lines	Customer Services	Contact and Coordination with Suppliers
Guarantee and Exchange	Store Layout	Markdowns	Interaction with Customers	Resupply, Promotional Suppliers
Customer Services	Public Relations	Markups	Merchandise Information	Delivery
Credit	Telephone Sales	Price/Perceived Quality	Salespeople's Advice	External Warehousing
Alterations and Adjustments	The Internet	Efficiency	Support People	In-Store Logistics
Delivery	Special Sales	Factors Affecting Prices	Maintenance	Inventory Control
Parking		Warehouses	Cleaning	Merchandise Movement
		Handling Goods	Security	Merchandise Location
		Computerized Controls	Delivery	Merchandise Combinations
				Internal Displays
				Window Displays
				Connection with Store Layout
STORE IMAGE	STORE IMAGE	STORE IMAGE	STORE IMAGE	STORE IMAGE

STORE IMAGE

Strategic Business Units vs. Profit Centers

The second consideration in strategy implementation is to evaluate the relative roles of and interaction between strategic business units (SBUs) and profit centers (PCs). SBUs and PCs are standard terms in both marketing and accounting books. However, these concepts are scarcely used in retailing. Nevertheless, they play a critical role in retailing for strategy implementation. All retailers, regardless of size, have strategic business units and profit centers. Both strategic business units and profit centers are comprised of groups of products or, in some cases, departments that have a common market base.

If there are managers of some of these special units, they typically have complete responsibility to integrate all of their functions into the retailing strategy to fulfill certain goals or compete with readily identifiable competitors (Samli 1998). The manager of the sporting goods department of Wal-Mart is certainly competing with similar departments in other discount department stores as well as with sporting goods stores (Samli and Shaw 2002).

SBUs are very critical in establishing a competitive advantage for a retail store. It is possible, for instance, that while a seafood market is known for the freshness of its products, a competitor may be well known for its lobster prices. Similarly, one supermarket is very well known for its deli center, whereas another is well known for its fresh produce center. These unique departments or product groups increase the store's outside reach and enhance its image. As a result, the store attracts more customers because of its increasing market outreach.

Profit centers, on the other hand, imply internal strength of the retail establishment. When the customers come in, they buy products from the profit centers, and these, in return, make a greater contribution to the profit picture. However, the critical issue here is that while some products or departments have more external or market appeal, others bring more money in. But quite often, if not most of the time, SBUs are not PCs; therefore, it is critical to decide the external strengths and the internal strengths of the store and how they could be balanced. Exhibit 7-3 illustrates interconnections between SBUs and PCs. As displayed in the exhibit, the upper left quadrant depicts the optimal situation. When certain product groups or departments are both SBUs and PCs, then the retailing activity is optimized. SBUs and PCs are synergistic. The opposite, of course, is the lower right

Exhibit 7-3. The Interaction Between SBUs and PCs

STRATEGIC BUSINESS UNIT

		GOOD CHOICE	POOR CHOICE
PROFIT CENTERS	GOOD CHOICE	Good management (balance between internal and external appeals)	Questionable management (too many internal, too few external appeals)
	POOR CHOICE	Borderline poor management (too many external, too few internal appeals)	Poor management (too few internal and external appeals)

Source: Adapted and revised from Samli, 1998.

quadrant. The retailer here does not know its internal or external strengths. There is no distinction made between SBUs and PCs. The end result is disaster. In the lower left quadrant, if the retailer survives and makes money, it will be in the long run. Without internal profit centers, it will not survive. On the other hand, the upper right quadrant is a short-run story. The retail establishment has good PCs, but it does not have external market power to bring customers in. If the customers are not coming in, they cannot patronize the profit centers. As can be seen, in implementing the retail strategic plan successfully, it is critical for the retailer to have the PCs and SBUs identified and well balanced. Consider the following: an independent department store in a Southeast university town has had a very busy small restaurant. One day the management shut it down. The reason was that the restaurant "was not yielding any profits." The department store management had never analyzed what the restaurant customers bought before or after eating. Thus the restaurant, an SBU, was eliminated without anyone assessing its contributions to the store's PCs (Samli and Shaw 2002). On a smaller scale, retailing PCs and SBUs may not be separate departments but separate product groups.

Store–Product Combinations

The third aspect of strategy implementation is creating the proper balance between the store and the product. In typical marketing books, three categories of consumer products are identified. These are convenience goods, shopping goods, and specialty goods. While the first group is purchased often, conveniently, and at low prices, the second group deals with expensive, high-ticket items without strong brand loyalty. Finally, the third group represents expensive, branded products where brand loyalty is very strong.

The same analogy can be used for retail stores as well. There are convenience stores, neighborhood ice cream parlors, video stores, barbershops, pizza places, and so on. There are shopping stores, such as Target or Sears, where people shop around for better prices and product selection. Finally, specialty stores are upscale jewelry stores, apparel stores, or upscale department stores, such as Neiman Marcus. The important consideration here is to make sure that the store–product combinations are just right. Exhibit 7-4 illustrates nine combinations of stores and products. Whereas convenience stores should not carry expensive jewelry, specialty stores should not carry disposable diapers. In the final analysis, sound retail strategy is trying to create store loyalty whenever possible, as in using strong product or brand loyalties.

As seen in Exhibit 7-4, situations 3, 6, and 9 show brand or product loyalty. Situations 7, 8, and 9, on the other hand, display strong store loyalty. Samli (1998, p. 187) proposes three conditions:

1. If the combinations are two degrees removed from each other, the result may be quite ineffective.
2. Instead of a single one of the nine cells, two side-by-side cells may be very appropriate.
3. The general positioning of the store is critical in the choice of these strategic cells.

As stated, if the classifications are two degrees removed, such as a convenience store selling specialty goods, in this case 7-Eleven selling fine jewelry, it will not spell success.

Illustrating point 2, a convenience store can sell some shopping goods along with convenience products. This can be rather effective.

Finally, positioning of the store needs to be considered first. If, for instance, a store enters the market where there is a well-known, very upscale store, then the new store may position itself slightly below the existing store. It is reasonable for this store to carry somewhat lower quality products. Without a proper balance between products and stores, it will be difficult to implement any strategic plan.

Exhibit 7-4. Strategic Alternatives Relating to Store-Product Combinations

STORE TYPES	CONVENIENCE GOODS	SHOPPING GOODS	SPECIALTY GOODS
Convenience Stores	(1) Convenience is the critical factor. Consumers buy whatever is available in the most accessible stores. *Brand loyalty and store loyalty do not exist.*	(2) Consumers will choose. There are at least perceived price and quality differences in the assortments. *Brand loyalty and store loyalty do not exist*	(3) Brands are very critical. Consumers may buy them at the most accessible store. *Brand loyalty exists.*
Shopping Stores	(4) Consumers shop at different stores in order to get the best service or the best price. But they are not influenced by the brand, product, or store. *Brand loyalty and store loyalty do not exist.*	(5) Consumers are likely to compare both stores and the merchandise mixes. They will try to buy the best price from the best store. *Some degree of brand recognition and store recognition exist.*	(6) Consumers are product and brand driven. But they will buy these from the best possible store. They will compare stores. *Some store recognition and strong brand loyalty exist.*
Specialty Stores	(7) Although they are indifferent to product or brand, consumers prefer to shop at a specific store. *Strong store loyalty exists.*	(8) Consumers are strongly attached to the store. But they will carefully examine and compare the products. *Strong store loyalty and some brand recognition exist.*	(9) Consumers strongly prefer the store as well as the product brand. *Both strong brand and store loyalty exist.*

Source: Adapted and revised from Samli, 1998.

PERFORMANCE EVALUATION

The last item in Exhibit 7-1 is performance evaluation. Particularly in retailing, there is not enough time to wait until the end of the calendar season or fiscal year. There must be a major effort to determine if the strategy is implemented properly and if it is working. Every retailer must develop early indicators of performance. It is difficult to create a list of early indicators for any and all retailers. However, it is reasonable to claim success if the newly introduced product line is well accepted or the store's advertising is bringing in people. Specific conditions that each retailer faces lend themselves to the establishment of very specific early indicators.

SUMMARY

In order to cater effectively to the chosen targets, the retailer must develop a strategic plan. However, as the strategy is being constructed, there are many segment modifiers. Five such modifiers are identified in this chapter.

The strategic options of a retailer are numerous. Seven key strategy options are identified and discussed in this chapter.

Finally, the planned strategy must be implemented. Three key areas of implementation are discussed in the chapter. The first is which retail mix, actually what combination of retail mixes, is necessary for different retailing strategies to be implemented. Second, a distinction between strategic business units (SBUs) and profit centers (PCs) is made. Then the balance between the two is discussed. Without such a balance, it will be impossible to implement the retail strategy. Finally, nine store–product combinations are identified. It is maintained here that unless a balance between the product and store combinations is achieved, it will be impossible to implement the retail strategy.

Finally, it is emphasized that performance evaluation is extremely critical. A retailer cannot wait until the financial results are obtained. It is critical for each retailer to develop certain early indicators so that performance can be evaluated quickly.

REFERENCES

Samli, A. Coskun (1998), *Strategic Marketing for Success in Retailing*, Westport, CT: Quorum Books.

Samli, A. Coskun, and Shaw, Eric (2002), "Achieving Managerial Synergism: Balancing Strategic Business Units and Profit Centers," *Journal of Market Focused Management*, January, 59–73.

8

Developing, Measuring, and Managing Store Image

A consumer entering Sam's or Costco certainly experiences different feelings from one entering Neiman Marcus or Saks Fifth Avenue. These feelings will be accentuated by ambiance, merchandise, service, and other store features (Samli 1998). Every retail store has a personality which is the sum total of impressions a consumer will receive as he or she enters the store and shops around. That atmosphere, which is called *store image*, may be very suitable for one customer and totally unsuitable for others.

Individuals do not face a new stimulus such as exploring a new store as if this were a completely novel experience. This idea is promoted by the category-based-processing theory which implies that a variety of experiential information modifies the intensity of the current experience and expectation (Samli 1998). Consumers will compare incoming information against the knowledge and/or experiences that they have stored in their memories.

Exhibit 8-1 illustrates how this theory works in reality. An individual who is familiar with Wal-Mart encounters a new Wal-Mart. The information imparted by the new Wal-Mart store in the form of promotion, ambiance, service,and so forth comes into play in comparison with past experiences with Wal-Mart.

A retail store is not only a place where goods and services are purchased, it is also a place where a combination of functional and emotional stimuli are perceived and acted upon. These functional and emotional stimuli are emitted through the store image (Samli 1998). Thus, a retail store has many personal and impersonal aspects that distinguish it from other stores. Each and every store, intentionally or unintentionally, emits many tangible and intangible stimuli that are synergistic. Thus, a retail store's functional qualities, physical attributes, and symbolic characteristics are all intertwined in the form of a store image.

Exhibit 8-1. The Theory of Encountering and Perceiving a Store Image

Step

1. The store must match a previously defined category of stores. (Oh! Here is the new Wal-Mart Store. I wonder how it compares to the other Wal-Marts I have seen.)

2. The store must give out cues that will match information about the category of store it belongs to. (The consumer enters. Well! It seems like just about the same merchandise and the same layout.)

3. If the store is perceived to match an existing category of stores, it means it activated the criteria to describe that category. (I wonder if this Wal-Mart is better in giving out information than others, so we can compare.)

4. If the set of criteria is activated, all the information is transferred to this store. (It appears that the salespeople here don't know much about consumer electronics, just as the others.)

5. If the set of criteria is activated, this set will determine the relevance and consistency of the information about the store. (Gee! This Wal-Mart is exactly the same as the others. I have had good experiences with Wal-Marts before.)

EVERY STORE HAS AN IMAGE

No retail establishment is all things to all people. As a store continues to perform, even if it has not done so deliberately, it will develop an image de facto. It is critical to realize that an image projected deliberately is always better than an image emerging after the fact. In deliberate attempts, the retailer is being proactive rather than reactive or inactive. As the store promotes its functional qualities and psychological attributes, it is projecting a synergistic image. The functional qualities are related to how well the store meets the aspirations of its target market by providing price, quality, product mix, service, and store logistics.

The store's psychological attributes are less tangible and more difficult to evaluate. Appealing to the psyche of consumers is extremely difficult, and the measurement of this appeal is even more difficult.

The store must be realistic and perhaps a little subtle as it makes deliberate statements such as:

- This is the friendliest place you have ever shopped.
- We have the best values for the most reasonable prices.
- Our cutting edge technology will transform your life.
- This is the ultimate destination for lingerie.

By definition, the image is projected and communicated through personal and impersonal communications in the form of a combination of tangible and intangible characteristics that provide an overall symbolic impression. This latter says, "Hey! This is what I am." Of course, if the store's claims and the customers' perceptions of the store do not match, then there is no possibility of creating differential congruence, which again is the essence of the store's competitive advantage.

In many ways strategic retailing can be described as developing and managing a store's image. Because store image is such a complex and synergistic phenomenon, the retailer must thoroughly master the concept. Only by doing so can the proactive retailer survive the retail jungle.

DIMENSIONS OF STORE IMAGE

If a retailer is to use store image as a key strategic weapon to achieve competitive advantage, the key components of store image must be known and prioritized. Thus the store image can be used to best advantage.

Exhibit 8-2 illustrates nine dimensions of store image. These dimensions carry different weights, depending on the choice of strategy and the way it is implemented by the retail establishment. A category killer, for instance, would emphasize the first dimension reported in the exhibit, which encompasses merchandise and pricing of the merchandise. However, a differentiator may find it more effective to promote and use the store atmosphere. If the store is positioned below the competitor's price range, it may emphasize all the physical aspects of the image as opposed to the store that is positioned above competition. The latter will have to use more psychological dimensions of the image.

Images vary not only by store type but also from one market segment to another. The retailer, obviously, must be able to understand, evaluate, and use key image dimensions so that a synergistic and effective image can be constructed and, if necessary, manipulated. All of these activities dwell upon measuring the current trends, events, and other forces that influence retail image.

IMAGE MEASUREMENT

In order to manage the image, it must be measured. Different techniques can be used to measure the store image; however, once the store image is measured in a specific way, then it must

Exhibit 8.2. The Key Dimensions of Store Image

DIMENSION	DESCRIPTION
Merchandise	There are at least five identifiable sub-dimensions: quality, selection or assortment, styling or fashion, guarantees, and pricing.
Service	The areas included in this dimension are: general service, salesclerk service, presence of self-service, ease of merchandise return, delivery service, and credit policies.
Clientele	Social class appeal, self-image congruence, and store personnel are included in this dimension.
Physical Facilities	The features included here are: elevators, lighting, air conditioning, washrooms, along with store layout, aisle placement, section identification, carpeting, and architecture.
Convenience	Three key sub-dimensions are identified: general convenience, location convenience, and parking.
Promotion	This group includes sales promotion, advertising, displays, coupons, symbols, and colors.
Store Atmosphere	This is an intangible category. Included are congeniality, customers' feelings, and ambience.
Institutional Factors	This is also an intangible category. It deals with reliability, reputation, and modernity.
Posttransaction Satisfaction	Included here are merchandise in use, returns and adjustments, receptiveness to complaints and other desires.

Source: Adapted and revised from Samli, 1998.

be continued to be measured in the same way so that there will be continuity of measurement, so as to reveal any expected or unexpected changes.

Exhibit 8-3 presents some important techniques used in store image measurement. Two types of measurement techniques are used for this purpose, unstructured and structured.

Unstructured Techniques

Four such techniques are presented in the exhibit. Word association is an old and widely used psychological technique. Free word association dealing with what comes to mind first as the store is mentioned could be rather effective.

Exhibit 8.3. Store Image Measurement

TECHNIQUES (Unstructured)	DESCRIPTION
Word Association	Trying to determine which word comes to mind in describing the store.
Sentence Completion	If I want to get the best value for the price I will go to...
Cartoon Test	Describe the customers that you see in the picture and what they are doing.
Open-Ended Questions	What do you like the most about shopping at XYZ Store?

TECHNIQUES (Structured)	DESCRIPTION
Semantic Differential	Locate us on the continuum: Modern ◄——► Old fashioned
Multidimensional Scaling	Comparing stores on a perceptual map
Multiattribute Models	Semantic differential with weights to establish relative importance of each factor
Multivariate Techniques	Highly quantitative, sophisticated techniques including clustering, discriminant analysis, factor analysis, and canonical analysis.

Source: Adapted and revised from Samli, 1998.

Sentence completion is used by marketing researchers perhaps more often. Completing the sentence presents the whole thought process that reflects the individual's thinking about the store.

The cartoon test is now commonly used. It may be able to bring up some deeper impressions about the store. How the test is designed and how it is interpreted are critical points in using this technique.

Open-ended questions are very practical and quite commonly used. Asking respondents about their impressions of the store and receiving their comments in their own words is a rather practical approach. The analysis of results may be rather difficult, however, since there may be many different responses. Thus, very strong interpretive skills may be required of the researcher.

Structured Techniques

The difference between "structured" and "unstructured" is related to the form of response. Whereas in unstructured techniques, the response is not formatted, and respondents can use their own approach for answers and verbal expressions, in the structured techniques, the response is formatted. This means that they are oriented more toward attitudinal scaling than toward open-ended motivational approaches. In other words, whereas the structured techniques have the tendency to measure attitudes, unstructured techniques can help bring to the surface motives that are, at least partially, subconscious. Studies have shown that identifying subconscious aspects of purchase behavior may shed light on new and unexpected dimensions about our store. In one such study, for instance, researchers uncovered that the store was a haven for shoplifting. That could not have been measured by structured techniques alone.

Semantic Differential: Of the four structured techniques that are listed in Exhibit 8-3, the semantic differential is the most common. Marketing scholars have traditionally used the semantic differential for many different aspects of store image evaluation. For instance, it has been used for measuring the impact of television advertising on a department store image or to determine the differences between symbolic and functional store images, among many other uses (Samli 1998).

The technique is easy to administer and tabulate. It also allows the presentation of the processed data in a format that is easily understood and visually formatted. It does not require extensive verbal skills on the part of respondents. They can respond rather easily. Additionally, the technique is considered to be quite reliable in the sense that the results are consistent under typical and similar conditions.

However, two problem areas are related to the semantic differential. First, the research needs to determine the attributes (or dimensions) of the store to be included in the measurement instrument. Second, we must assess the relative importance of these attributes and how they are related to each other, that is, to what extent these store characteristics are inter-related and how they contribute to the overall store image (Samli 1998).

Multidimensional Scaling: Multidimensional scaling (MDS) is a newer and somewhat more sophisticated tool that is used to measure store image. It also is versatile enough to be used in different aspects of store image measurements. MDS makes the fewest possible assumptions regarding the respondent's reaction. Furthermore, it provides the respondent an opportunity to make the fewest possible judgments. As a result of these special features in using MDS, respondents can be objective in a very subjective attitudinal questioning process. The process can help management evaluate the store's image in comparison with a competitor's image. This is not a very simple technique to administer and analyze, however.

Multiattribute Models: These models attempt to rectify the major deficiencies in the semantic differential method. In the semantic differential, all of the variables are given the same weight. What if, for example, in the case of Store A, location is not as important as the merchandise mix or price mix? The semantic differential fails to point out this very important bit of information, but a multiattribute model will.

Marketers have been using this technique since it was developed by Fishbein in 1967. The technique enables the researcher to determine which store attributes are particularly important (salience) and their respective degrees of importance (valence). As a result, multiattribute models accomplish more than the semantic differential. However, it also has some of the same problems that the semantic differential has: specification of application of the model, since there are some major variations in the application of the model, and attribute generation in terms of deciding which variables or dimensions are going to be used in the model.

Multivariate Techniques: A variety of techniques fit under this title (Samli 1996). They are all geared for different types of analysis of the same phenomenon. The description of each technique is beyond the scope of this book. However, it can be simply stated that clustering can, for instance, profile loyal customers of the store, which is an indirect way of measuring the store image. Discriminant analysis can distinguish the characteristics of the key specific features of two competing stores. Factor analysis identifies whether there are certain hidden factors that might influence store loyalty, and canonical analysis verifies, for example, the presence of multiple store image definitions and their important factors. Even though these are quite powerful techniques, they have not been used extensively in retailing research (Samli 1998).

MANAGING THE IMAGE

There is not much value in spending time and effort to measure the store image if we cannot manage it. In fact, it is reasonable to posit that managing the retail store well is managing its image effectively. A well-managed store image enhances the probability of retail success by communicating a strong image in the store's target market. This would lead to increased sales and profitability. The retailer's repeat business is a major strength, and it is a function of a well-managed store image. Additionally, the store image interacts with product or brand images synergistically and can provide additional value to the product. Studies have shown that products in an upscale store have a more favorable image than the same products in a lower-scale store. Other studies have indicated that store image is used by consumers as a method of risk reduction. If the consumers believe in the store where they are shopping, then they feel more confident about the product (Samli 1998).

From our discussion thus far, it is clear that the retailer must have a proactive approach to constructing and managing the store's image. Exhibit 8-4 presents a five-step image management model. These five steps are the following: evaluate the current store image, establish a reference point, determine the changes to be made in the current image, implement and evaluate the changes that have been introduced, and relate the image changes to the store's performance.

A floor covering store (selling carpeting, rugs, and other such supplies) tried to find out if it should go more heavily into discounting. Following the five steps led to these conclusions:

- The current store image indicated that it was respected as a "classy" place.
- Its key competitor was a discounter clearly appealing to a different class of clientele.
- The store decided to play up its classy status.
- As a classy store it provided more advice for interior decoration and a slightly higher quality merchandise mix.
- The store found out that the reinforcement of the current image worked well and it stayed away from discounting.

Evaluating the Current Store Image

If we don't understand the current image, we cannot improve upon it. Understanding the current image begins with its

Exhibit 8-4. Store Image Management Paradigm

STEPS	FUNCTIONS
Step 1 Evaluate the current store image	• Define the store image • Identify its important dimensions and their respective importance • Measure the current image according to the first two functions
Step 2 Establish a reference point	• Evaluate the image of a key competitor • Identify its strengths • Establish the relative importance of each strength
Step 3 Determine the changes to be made in the current image	• Identify the store's strengths and weaknesses • Decide where changes need to take place • Compare the desired changes and the expected direction of the store
Step 4 Implement and evaluate the changes that have been introduced	• Identify specifically each change that has been implemented • Evaluate the impact of these changes vis-à-vis the key competitor • Critically decide if the new changes should continue
Step 5 Relate the image changes to the store performance	• Measure the changes in sales and market share • Remeasure customers' store loyalty • Contrast the changes between loyal customers and new customers • Evaluate changes in profitability

Source: Adapted and revised from Samli, 1998.

definition. If and when it is properly defined, its important variables surface. Identifying the image variables or dimensions and determining their relative importance in the form of their contribution to the overall image would indicate the strengths and weaknesses of the existing image. In this step there could be serious alternatives as far as introducing other image dimensions, eliminating or reducing some of the existing ones, or redirecting and re-emphasizing others. It is quite possible that by using the multiattribute analysis, the retailer may find that the employees' knowledge level is much more critical than the store's price level policy. The retailer, therefore, has the option of keeping this feature as it is, strengthening it by providing more training for the employees, or promoting this feature more readily, to mention just a few courses of action.

Establish A Reference Point

The decisions relating to which image dimensions to keep and which ones to modify will be partially dependent on the reference points that are established. The reference points can be established by evaluating the image of a key competitor. Once the competitor's strengths are identified and their relative importance is approximated, then it becomes rather important for our retailer to decide if it wants to be a deviator, imitator, complementer, or innovator (see Chapter 1) vis-à-vis this competitor.

Determine the Changes to be Made

Based on the above two steps, it is possible to decide on the store's strengths and weaknesses. It is critical here to decide what (if any) changes must be implemented in reconstructing and projecting the image. Clearly, the changes implemented in the store image are likely to take the store in an expected and/or hoped-for direction. Of course, the research may show that the store is very strong in its target markets. Hence, rather than changing or slightly modifying the current image, reinforcing it may be the best alternative. This implies that the existing image features are more important and more effective than others.

Implement and Evaluate

After a retailer comes to understand the store's weaknesses and strengths and decide on what changes in the image are likely to be initiated, implementation becomes critical. The difference between the previous image and the currently revised image needs to be carefully examined. Here image-related research data are necessary. The store may be able to conduct a before/after analysis. In such analysis, it is critical that these two sets of data be comparable. In order for the two sets of data to be comparable, the data-collection techniques, data-collection instruments, and data-analysis methodology must be totally consistent.

Once the previous image and the new image are compared—within the constraints of validity and reliability of the data generated—it should become obvious that the attempts to improve the image have been successful. As the previous and the new images are compared, it must be evident that the current image is succeeding in the direction that the changes were intended to produce. For instance, customers indicated that a better store layout was much desired. However, if, after the store layout has been changed, the reaction is that the new one is not even as good as the old one, then the difference is not in the direction that was intended. It is clear that the direction and the intensity of the changes as a result of the implemented new strategy must be quickly and accurately measured.

Relate Image Changes to the Performance

The changes in the image must be reflected in the store's performance; otherwise the store is wasting time, effort, and resources. Thus, the success of the first four steps in Exhibit 8-4 can only be realistically determined from the fifth step. The market performance of the retail store is the ultimate measure of store image management. There are at least four different ways to measure the store's market performance. First, changes in sales volume and market share can be measured and compared with the same period in the past. Second, the change in the degree of store loyalty can be evaluated. Third, the store outreach is assessed by examining if the store is attracting customers from further distances. And finally, the profitability of the store can be utilized as the key criterion of performance. It is clear that the market performance is improving if the improvements in the image are bringing in more profits. Going back to an earlier theme, differential congruence is being reinforced and further strengthened if the image management effort is working well.

DIFFERENTIAL CONGRUENCE REVISITED

As we develop and manage the store image, we must make sure that it is acceptable to our target market. This is how differential congruence is developed and strengthened. Differential congruence gives viability to a retail establishment and reinforces its probability of success. In order to achieve differential congruence, a harmony between the store image and the individual customer's self-image is required. Through its efforts to project a store image, the retailer claims the presence of certain features that are unique to the store, which then differentiates it from others. Above all, these store features are consistent with the store customers' self-image. The congruence between these two images leads to greater long-term customer satisfaction and resultant customer loyalty. The value derived from patronizing the retail establishment translates into profit for the retailer.

It is critical to restate that the store image is a product of the store's functional and psychological (emotional) features. These two groups of features lead to a symbolic store image. Early research studies mostly concentrated on the store's functional features. We see, then, a gap in research findings relating to a store's emotional (psychological) features and resultant symbolic features that represent the total store personality.

The symbolic, value-expressive store image deals with generalities such as traditional versus modern, high status versus low status, pleasant atmosphere versus unpleasant atmosphere, and the like. If a consumer perceives that, on the basis of its functional and psychological features, a store is patronized by primarily high-class consumers and that person also sees himself as a high-class consumer, then there will be congruence as intended, and that consumer is likely to develop store loyalty. Needless to say, store loyalty means repeat sales and repeat sales make a difference between surviving and not surviving in retailing. Creating such a congruence with its customers in its trading area indicates that the store has created a differential advantage. In its customers' minds the store is different from others, and shopping there is a pleasant experience because the store has a symbolic image that is very consistent with the individual's own self-image.

DISCREPANCY BETWEEN MANAGEMENT AND CUSTOMER PERCEPTION

In trying to establish congruence, analyzing customers' perceptions of the store image compared to management's perception of the store image can be an important diagnostic tool. Such analysis may indicate, for instance, that customers think the store is not modern, whereas management thinks it is; similarly, customers may think that parking is very bad while management may not agree; or customers may think that the store's credit policy is inadequate, while management believes it is outstanding. Such discrepancies can be used for diagnostic analysis. Out of such diagnostic efforts Exhibit 8-5 emerges.

The upper left quadrant of Exhibit 8-5 illustrates the ideal situation. Differential congruence of the store is strong, and most of the congruence features indicate the true strength of the store. Both management and customers agree on these positive features.

The lower left quadrant illustrates a rather interesting situation. Here there are special strengths of the store that were not known up to that point. Customers think that some features of the store are better than what management realizes. These special strengths must be further used in terms of advertising and other promotions to achieve congruence.

The upper right quadrant is a critical problem situation. It appears that customers do not expect much from the store, but they do not see themselves in a favorable light either. Hence there is congruence, but in a negative manner. The store may be appealing to the wrong target and is in a very stagnant situation. Much managerial creativity is needed here to turn this whole situation around.

The lower right quadrant of Exhibit 8-5 indicates that a number of problems undetected earlier have surfaced and need to be taken care of. The store has much work ahead if it wants to be successful. The greater the discrepancy between the two groups, customers and store management, the greater the severity of the problem that needs to be resolved quickly. In essence, this

Exhibit 8-5. Discrepancy Between Management and Customer Perception

	IN FAVOR OF THE STORE	*CRITICAL DEFICIENCY*
CONGRUENCE	Competitive advantage features. True strengths of the store. Both groups are in agreement positively.	Store has congruence with the wrong target market and the characteristics appealing to that target.
INCONGRUENCE	Unknown competitive advantage features that should be used for further promotion. Customers think the store is better than what management thinks.	Surfacing problems undetected up to now. They need very special attention immediately. Customers think some problems are very critical

situation indicates that the store management is not even aware of the existing problems. Certainly, unless some dramatic changes take place, the store is not likely to survive.

An Illustration

Upon an analysis of customers' and management's evaluation of the store, a small gift shop adjacent to a major university in a small Southeastern town realized that it belonged in the lower right quadrant of Exhibit 8-5. Analysis indicated that the store had limited variety, limited stock for the products it had, and a confusing atmosphere because the store was run by part-time help who did not know how to organize the store and its inventory. This whole scenario was not fully detected by the management until recently. Management laid out a series of strategic alternatives:

- Having more and better-trained full-time staff to help serve customers with a more appealing merchandise mix. Cater to students more by making the store more student-friendly.

- Make the store more nonstudent-oriented. Change the store's image somewhat, adjust the merchandise mix accordingly, and appeal to young adults in town.

- Develop the store and its atmosphere to appeal to the upper middle class, with significantly improved ambience, merchandise mix, and general orientation. Establishing a name outside of town to attract more out-of-towners.

Although all three strategic alternatives appeared to be attractive, the first one seemed most doable with less risk, since the university is growing and students have more discretionary income. It also appeared that since the current target market consists of students, alternatives 2 and 3 would not create differential congruence and move the store from the lower right quadrant to the upper left quadrant in Exhibit 8-5.

Implementing alternative 1, however, is not as simple as it may seem. There are many details to take care of which are likely to strengthen the store further in its niching strategy. The management ponders the possibility of expanding the merchandise mix more in the direction of coeds, developing a more liberal return policy, and implementing certain tactics of grouping the new merchandise in a dorm-room arrangement and displaying the most attractive new lines in the best possible manner. Such a proactive approach to differential congruence development is bound to get good results. Of course, the management should have contingency plans in case the strategy implementation does not work as well as expected.

ALL MUST END UP IN STORE LOYALTY

Our discussion thus far indicates that in retailing we are selling a store image. If that image is consistent with the target group's self-image, the store will have a good chance of succeeding. But, in order to develop a congruence between customers' self-image and the store image, the retailer must identify demographics, psychographics, geographics, shopping habits, and media habits of the target market, among other information.

Differential congruence, if successful, generates store loyalty. Determining store loyalty, therefore, is critical in terms of providing direction for the store management. Just what are the indicators of the presence of store loyalty? There are a number of them. A brief discussion of such indicators follows:

If, for instance, customers visit the store often, it indicates loyalty. Similarly, if the store customers do not shop around much before entering our store, it would indicate the same thing. Just what proportion of the customers' total purchases of the product categories the store sells are purchased by the customer in the store?

If, for instance, 30 percent of a customer's apparel purchases are done in the store, that customer is more loyal than the one who purchases 10 percent of her total apparel acquisitions. If the customer displays a preference for the store by choosing it on every possible occasion, then there is reasonable loyalty. The customer may have definite intentions to come back, which is a good indicator of loyalty. The customer may live in the area and be loyal to the area and/or the shopping complex where the store is located. In this instance, store loyalty is a natural outcome. Finally, the extent to which the consumer recommends the store to friends is a measure of loyalty.

It must be posited that many of the points made in this chapter require up-front information as well as follow-up information in the form of feedback. It is strongly suggested that attempts to gather data and generate information are not just big-time research that only large-scale retailers are involved in. In fact, small retailers need research-generated information even more.

Understanding research, evaluating the need for it, and particularly knowing how to use it are very critical for small retailers. Their well-being depends on it.

SUMMARY

Image is the sum total of all of the impressions emanating from a store. All retail stores have an image. Managing a retail store well is managing its image. Image has multiple dimensions. Nine such dimensions are discussed in this chapter. The techniques used to measure store image are briefly discussed. These techniques are classified into two groups—unstructured and structured. At times, the use of more than one technique may be necessary.

A five-step store image management process is presented in the chapter. The process allows changes to be made in the existing image of the store. The chapter re-emphasized the fact that a successful retail establishment has a strong differential congruence which is closely related to image management. Successful differential congruence leads to customer loyalty, and there are multiple factors that can be used to measure store loyalty. The retailer must be able to conduct and use research for all of the important objectives laid out in this chapter.

REFERENCES

Fishbein, Martin (1967), "A Behavior Theory Approach to the Relations Between Beliefs About An Object and the Attitude Towards That Object," in *Readings in Attitude Theory and Measurement*, New York: John Wiley and Sons.

Samli, A. Coskun (1998), *Strategic Marketing for Success in Retailing*, Westport, CT: Quorum Books.

Samli, A. Coskun (1996), *Information Driven Marketing Decisions*, Westport, CT: Quorum Books.

9

People Are Our Strength

In essence, retailing is people business. Officially, *relationship marketing* was not generated in the retailing sector, but it was widely practiced by the retailing sector long before it became an important concept in marketing literature. All consumers end up in retail stores sooner or later. Without proper people a suitable atmosphere of warm and effective human interaction cannot exist, and the retail establishment cannot survive. Thus, people are our major strength, particularly in small retail establishments. As a result, without appropriate human resource management, the probabilities of success for our store will be nil.

Perhaps the most important point that needs to be made in this chapter is that human resource management is not simply an administrative process in retailing. Rather, particularly in small and medium-sized retailing, it is a strategic tool. This is why earlier we introduced human resources as one of the five retail mixes, key strategic tools. The retailer should not think of human resource management as any less important than the promotional efforts or pricing practices and the like. In fact, a small retailer that cannot distinguish itself from other similar retailers in any other way can rely on the store's human resources to make a difference.

More than 20 million people, representing about 17 percent of the national labor force, are typically employed by the retailing sector. Not only do all indications point to a continuing growth in retail employment, but, additionally, if the country continues to lose manufacturing jobs, this void is going to be remedied by even more retailing and service jobs.

Despite the volume and growth of its human resources, the retailing sector is experiencing serious problems in employee performance and employee turnover. Unfortunately, the retailing sector does not always choose the best employees, train them well, or compensate them adequately so they will stay with a particular store. The employee turnover rate in this sector is the highest of all sectors. The average job tenure is estimated to be around 2.7 years, whereas the national average for all jobs is about 4.4 years. If we consider the costs of recruiting, hiring, and training new people, this statistic is alarming.

EXPECTATIONS OF RETAIL EMPLOYEES

All of the functions listed in the human resource mix presented in Exhibit 7-2 must be performed well. Retail employees will be engaged in personal selling and sales promotion, customer services, and interaction with customers. All of these imply willingness and ability on the part of the employees. Almost above all, employees must have excellent merchandise and service knowledge. As a result, they should be able to advise customers on a large variety of merchandise selection and on care, repair, return, and the like. Retail employees are support people. They not only make the place more attractive by maintaining and cleaning it, but also by performing other duties—delivery, assembly, and providing security. All of these functions reflect on the store image and are extremely important for the well-being of the retail establishment. It is therefore clear that a highly competent and highly motivated group of employees must do their best so that the retail establishment can generate maximum customer value, which translates into profit. In order for the human resource mix to be a strategic tool of competitive advantage, there must be a major human resource management activity in the retail establishment.

HUMAN RESOURCE MANAGEMENT

In a gigantic market, such as the one that exists in the United States, which includes a bombardment of product information upon the consumer, there is a tendency for product assortments in various retail outlets to become more and more similar. Eckerd, for instance, carries many standard grocery items, whereas many health, beauty and pharmaceutical items are found in Winn-Dixie. Since the product mixes are less differentiated, it is necessary for retailers to find other means of differentiation leading to differential congruence. Employee performance, generated by human resource management, is becoming more critical in creating such a needed differentiation. In many retail establishments, customer satisfaction is becoming predicated upon customer perception of employee performance. This point becomes even more critical in small-scale retailing where individual retailers can accomplish much by connecting with their customers. In the early and mid-1990s, Nordstrom Stores utilized the human resource mix to their advantage. Nordstrom employees were expected to go out of their way to serve their customers. They were willing and, perhaps, expected to make home deliveries, run simple errands, and obtain information about numerous retailing-related activities (Samli 1998).

Perhaps more than ever before, time is a major constraint in today's retailing. Consumers in general and customers specifically want to be served by employees as quickly as possible with the required level of service. If consumers are in a hurry, they may pay a premium for convenience. However, retailers may seek ways to offer customers more time efficiency as a competitive advantage through better trained and more efficient employees. In these cases, not only are the employees of retail stores directly in touch with customers, they also receive useful suggestions from them. As can be seen, the importance of the human resource mix is a powerful strategic tool in retailing.

In order to develop sound human resources, the retailer must deal with four extremely critical areas: search process, training, development, employee loyalty and trust. Exhibit 9-1 illustrates the human resource management process in retailing.

Search Process

Locating, acquiring, training, motivating, and, above all, retaining qualified employees is essential for effective retailing performance. Retailers must have a way of establishing the attributes and characteristics of their employees so that these workers will be *competent performers*. Once the criteria for competent performers are established, then the retailer must develop reliable sources of employees. These sources must be continuously evaluated in terms of the quality of the employees they are supplying. Of course, this evaluation process revolves around how well the retail employees are performing.

Although sound recruitment is essential for the health of retail operations, retailers, particularly small retailers, are handicapped in their ability to locate and attract quality personnel. Despite its might and far-reaching impact since almost every fifth person is employed in the retailing sector, this particular industry has a long-standing negative reputation. It pays very low salaries, the benefits it gives are kept to a minimum, the hours it requires are long or specifically arranged to be part-time, and its working conditions are not considered very pleasant. Despite all these

Exhibit 9-1. Human resource Management in Retailing

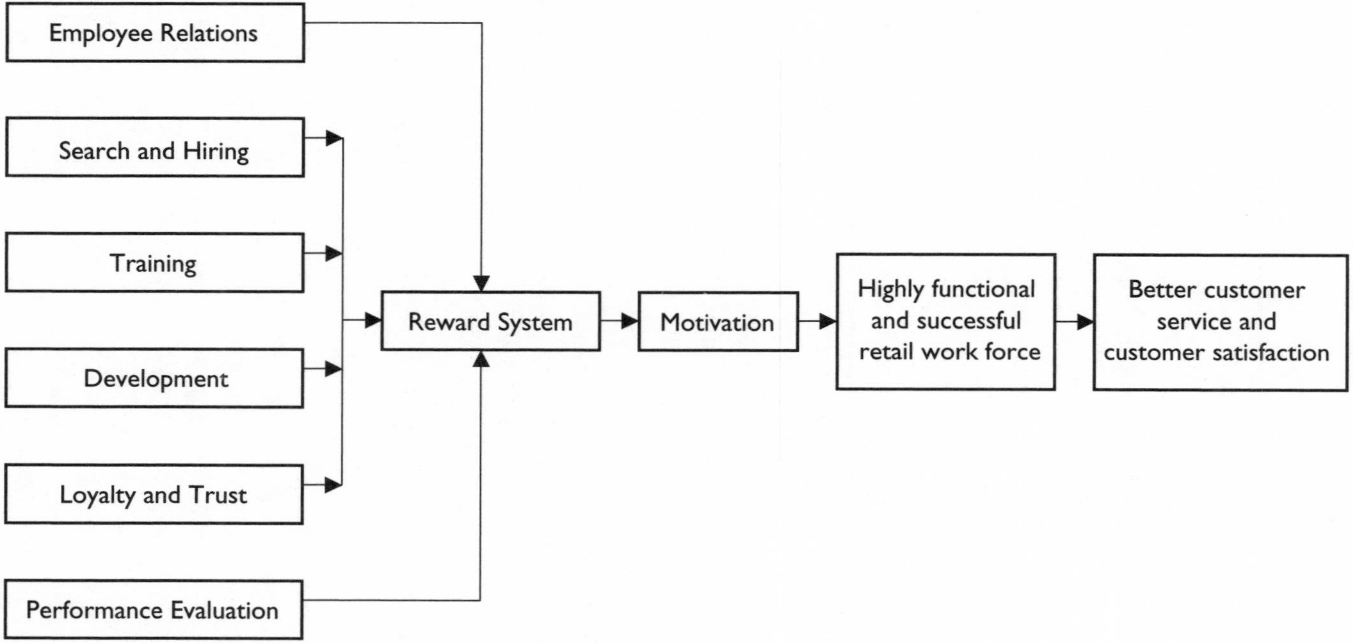

Better customer service and customer satisfaction

Highly functional and successful retail work force

Motivation

Reward System

Employee Relations

Search and Hiring

Training

Development

Loyalty and Trust

Performance Evaluation

Source: Adapted and revised from Samli and Ongan, 1996.

negative features, retail employees have extensive customer contact. If the employees are not happy, these customer contact hours may not be very productive for the retailer. If the employees are not happy, they are not likely to go out of their way to make customers happy (Samli 1998).

Retailing, as a profession, suffers from a critical image problem. Research has shown, time and again, that college students rate retailing near the bottom in their occupational preference list. Such an image problem does not encourage quality employees and prospective managers to seek a career in retailing.

Many retailers, particularly small retailers, lack the resources to develop an effective human resource management system. They cannot afford, for example, to systematically recruit, screen, and train prospective personnel. Particularly in small retailing, the manager's time is taken up by daily operational problems. Despite the fact that many crises originate from personnel-related issues, there simply is not enough time or strong inclination to develop powerful strategic human resource planning.

There is a bias on the part of retail managers that everyone must start at the bottom and work his or her way up. This mentality does not encourage the best possible talent to seek a career in retailing. Additionally, part of the bias is related to the fact that employee turnover is so high that some managers feel as if they are training people for other retailers. Hence they may not put their best effort forward in training newly hired personnel. All of these considerations indicate the problematic nature of retail human resource management.

Training

Retailing, in general, does not do a good job of training employees. Expenditures set aside for training are the lowest of any sector in our economy, in absolute as well as relative terms. For instance, the new training technology that is available through satellite communication systems is not used in retailing, except by a few select retailers,. Not only are retailers reluctant to invest in training for employees originally, but more advanced training, which is necessary as employees become more seasoned, is even less emphasized. Thus, the retailer cannot find its core competency area for want of competent performers. The industry-wide practice is "on-the-job training," which is unsystematic, disorganized, and quite ineffective. There is also a prevailing concept among retailers that needs to be questioned. Many retailers are hesitant to train their employees well for fear they will not stay with the company and may go join the competition.

Perhaps one of the most important problems in retail human resource management that is not well understood is that inadequate search and training *leads to* employee turnover, which, in itself, is likely to be more costly than better screening and training programs. After all, constantly finding new people and providing them with even minimal orientation is costly and time-consuming. During that wasted time, many potential sales transactions are likely to be missed.

It is ironic that whereas the human resource mix is so critical for the retailer's differential advantage, human resource management systems are not well developed. The relationship among training, turnover rate, and labor costs must be understood by retail managers if significant improvement is to occur in this area.

Development

Earlier a reference was made to continuity. Employees, in time, must be formed into good, flexible, knowledgeable, and helpful retail associates. Proper selection and training are necessary ingredients of this formation, but these by themselves are not totally adequate. It is necessary to develop a type of atmosphere within which retail employees can grow professionally. There may be formal or informal in-house activities to provide the employees with additional required skills as the nature of the industry changes. With the proliferation of technologically complex products and advanced systems and procedures employed by retailers, employees must be more and more equipped with special skills. They must feel that management is dedicated to improving their skill-based performance by providing ongoing opportunities to learn.

Loyalty and Trust

Since the human resource mix is a critical tool of the retailer in generating differential advantage, employee loyalty and dedication are critical for the retailer if it hopes to achieve satisfactory performance in its market segment. It may be maintained that a prerequisite to employee loyalty is the presence of mutual trust. This latter cannot be accomplished unless an aura of fairness, understanding, and honesty is present. Such an aura is quite likely to enhance employee job satisfaction and resultant performance. Of course, it is critical that both management and employees make an effort in this direction. Some experts believe that the empowerment of employees to use their own discretion in dealing with customers is likely to enhance customer value generation. A corporate culture that would encourage retail employees to feel they are part of the total picture and use their discretion in certain decision-making situations is very desirable. If the retail organization encourages and allows the exercise of discretion, the employees may put forth even greater effort toward customer satisfaction.

PUTTING A SYSTEM TOGETHER

A functional human resource management system must concentrate on three major areas: employee relations, performance evaluation, and a reward system (Exhibit 9-1). These three elements combined lead to the essence of human resource management in retailing: motivation. Exhibit 9-1 clarifies these focal points.

Employee Relations

A combination of policies, guidelines, and procedures used by the retailer that describes its responsibilities towards its employees and employees' responsibilities towards the retail establishment must be developed. Successful retailers have managed to connect their integrated benefit packages directly to the performance of their employees. These benefit packages are composed of intangible benefits such as recognition, as well as tangible benefits such as financial rewards. American retailing is rather behind Japan or Europe in putting together such comprehensive packages that are desirable by both parties. American retailers have not yet developed routine procedures for their employees that deal with career pathing, career enrichment, skills enhancement, flex-time, and team-building issues in general (Samli 1998). These are important issues in employee relations. It would be extremely desirable for retailers to become more sophisticated in these areas. Solid employee relations systems including all of these issues are likely to improve the retailer's overall performance. Thus, human resources must be treated as a major asset for the establishment rather than simply a cost factor.

Performance Evaluation

Fewer than half of the retailers in the United States are estimated to have a systematic approach to evaluating employees (Samli

1998). This is a rather low proportion that needs to be improved. Without a performance evaluation system, employees do not know what is expected of them; furthermore, it is difficult to inform them as to management's perception of their performance, and the employees' perceptions of how they are evaluated is blurred. Here, clearly stated job descriptions combined with carefully stated reward systems would be very effective.

Reward System

The reward system in the retailing sector is not what it should be. Retailers, in general, do not have good compensation systems that typically reward the best performers. Additionally, the whole sector pays less than the average pay by the private sector. The lack of an overall attractive reward system makes it difficult to stimulate a good feeling of belonging among the employees in the sector. Since, much of the time, the employees who are really effective and productive go unnoticed, they may become disheartened and leave. Thus, there is a major issue of the lack of behavior modification of the employees through using positive reinforcement. In fact, it may be stated that in retailing at this point in time, there is more negative reinforcement than positive. The employee, for instance, may not be praised for good performance, but will be admonished for bad performance. If employee pay is put at risk, which is a recent practice to stimulate harder work, and if the pay is to be more closely related to performance, then some latitude may be given to the employees to satisfy customers, which must also be considered. This connection is named *enfranchisement* (Schlesinger and Heskett 1991). This is a way of granting more freedom and responsibility to retail employees that may improve sales and earnings, while requiring less direct supervision from corporate management and providing increased employee earnings, job satisfaction, and employee retention. There is enough indication that these complex and vital relationships need to be explored further for the retailing sector to become more attractive as a career option and a generator of consumer value.

MOTIVATION

All of our discussion in this chapter leads in the direction of motivation. Without properly motivated workers, the human resource mix is not likely to create the needed differential advantage. Individuals working in retailing must be motivated to work both harder and smarter. This means better service for the consumer and greater consumer value generation. The reward system in retailing is the key motivator. Unless the reward system is brought up to a normal level, consistent with other sectors, the retailing sector may not perform up to its potential. Reiterating what has been said in the chapter, the reward system and performance must have a strong relationship. Thus, motivation will lead to the presence of a highly functional and successful retail work force.

CONNECTING PEOPLE AND SERVICE

Every retailer must ask this question: "Are our customers satisfied with our performance?" Performance here refers to service as well as to merchandise. Our people in retailing must exhibit reliability, responsiveness, assurance, and empathy.

In this context reliability implies providing services that we claim we provide. Responsiveness means keeping our customers informed about the services we are providing. Assurance implies courteous employees making customers feel safe and confident about their transactions. Finally, empathy stands for giving our customers the attention that they expect and deserve. Our employees must understand our customers' needs (Berman and Evans 2002). In small and medium-sized businesses particularly, there may not be a more critical factor to differentiate the store from its competition than service delivered by the employees of the store.

MANAGING QUALITY IN RETAILING

Retailers must build successful teams. Building successful teams, by definition, includes good hiring, good communications, and developing a reward system leading to motivation. Without motivation, retail success is likely to be less than satisfactory. However, traditional practices are such that a majority of retail managers operate under a "Theory X" orientation. Such an orientation includes strict supervision, narrow spans of control, reluctance to delegate, and generally exercising an adversarial relationship. The retailer needs to experiment with job enrichment programs, flex-time, employee incentive programs, and other creative and unconventional activities. Such programs will foster active employee participation in long-term planning, more flexibility in decision making, and enhanced individualism.

All of our discussion in this chapter is particularly important for small retailers who may not have much more than their personnel that can create a differential advantage. In recent years, small retailers have started using placement service professionals, who may prove to be extremely valuable in attracting the right type of employees to the establishment. These placement service professionals evaluate the retail store environment and what kind of match the new employees will create as they work for the retail establishment.

SUMMARY

Developing a human resource mix in retailing is critical, since this mix is an important competitive tool for the retail establishment. However, the retailing sector does not have a very good reputation for taking care of its employees, and hence, is suffering from a very high rate of disruptive employee turnover.

The retailer must understand the importance of searching and hiring the right people, giving them good training, keeping them longer, and helping them to develop further, thereby generating loyalty and mutual trust. All of these efforts lead to a three-point human resource management program concentrating on employee relations, performance evaluation, and a reward system. This three-point program will provide the basis for proper motivation,which is extremely critical for the human resource mix to be a powerful competitive tool.

REFERENCES

Berman, Berry, and Evans, Joel R. (2002), *Retail Management,* Upper Saddle River, NJ: Prentice Hall.

Samli, A. Coskun (1998), *Strategic Marketing for Success in Retailing,* Westport, CT: Quorum Books.

Samli, A. Coskun, and Ongan, N. Mehmet (1996), "Retail Human Resource Management: An Exploration and Research Agenda," *Journal of Marketing Channels,* September, 81-99.

Schlesinger, Leonard A., and Heskett, James L. (1991), "Enfranchisement of Service Workers," *California Management Review,* Summer, 83-99.

10

We Must Communicate
With Our Market

I have seen the attitude on the part of some retailers of "Well, they know we are here, and they will come." Actually, just because we are here does not mean success. As was discussed earlier in the book, if we want to develop and manage a store image, we must communicate that image to our target market. A deliberate and carefully calculated communication plan certainly takes speculations, rumors, and questionable gossip out of circulation and replaces them with the type of information and bits of fact that help construct our image in the minds of our customers and prospective customers. Such an activity further reinforces the image we are trying to develop. Without communication, there is a reasonable doubt that we can successfully construct and project the image that we believe will enhance our competitive advantage. The image of a retail store is the sum total of impressions perceived by different constituencies. The development and manipulation of that image cannot be achieved without communication. When the retailer wants to generate certain impressions about the store, then a communication activity that is carefully calculated and tightly controlled will have to be planned and executed.

IMPORTANCE OF RETAIL COMMUNICATION

All retailers have an image, but its emergence should not be left to luck. Proactivity in the communication process is one of the key ingredients of success in retailing. No retailer can survive as a well-kept secret. Similarly, no retailer can afford to wait and see how word-of-mouth communication among consumers is going to shape up. This author has seen many retail stores come into existence where the owner-managers would simply sit there and hope customers would come in. This type of "build it and they will come" mentality is extremely dangerous. A small gift shop concentrating on imports from Latin America, for instance, was opened in a small, sophisticated university town where the tastes and incomes would make a good niche market. However, it had two big problems: because of cost factors, the store located in a relatively less-developed part of town; moreover, there was no budget for advertising. People neither saw it nor did they know it existed. Those who had learned about the store had formed wrong impressions. The end result was a dismal failure.

Image development begins with promotion. Image manipulation (if needed) is also accomplished through promotion (Exhibit 10-1). Image development results in enhancement of name recognition. In a survey, it was found that less than one percent of the respondents knew the name and the nature of the Latin gift shop discussed above. If the store's name recognition is advanced, the attitude of its customers is likely to change for the better. The store's target market customers will be more attached

Exhibit 10-1. The Impact of Retail Communication

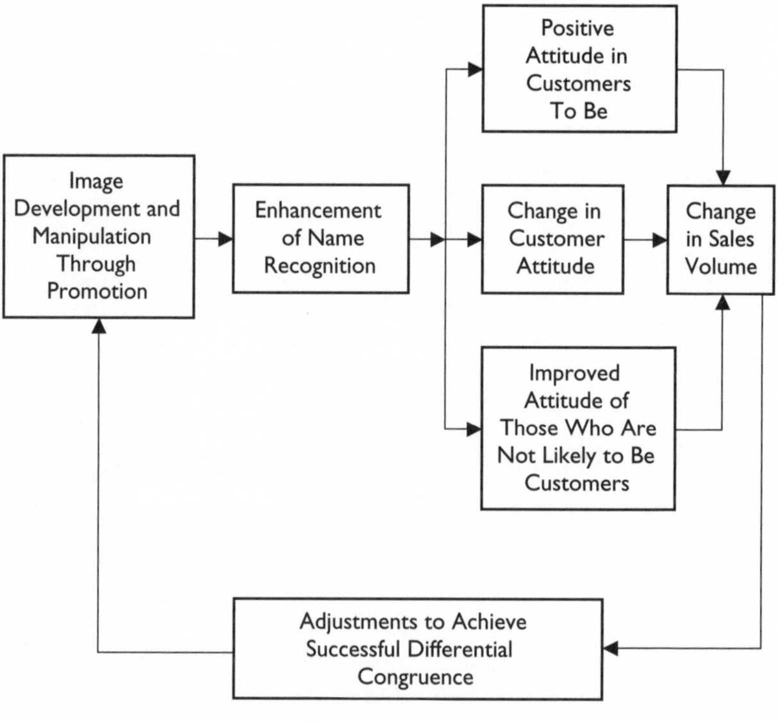

Source: Adapted and revised from Samli, 1998.

to it. Positive attitude may also spill over into the submarket of those who might be more interested in the store if they knew more. Finally, enhanced name recognition may even spill over into the segments of the market that are not likely to be customers of the store, at least in the near future. All of these direct and indirect results of successful promotion of the store's image result in increased sales volume and more customer loyalty. Of course, if results do not show the expected degree of improvement in sales volume and customer loyalty, additional research may take place to further modify the image and its promotion. Thus, Exhibit 10-1 presents an adjustment mechanism or feedback to modify the image in a manner that will be more effective in establishing a differential congruence for the store.

MANAGING THE PROMOTIONAL ACTIVITY

Although communicating with the market revolves around and ends up being a part of store image, often efforts to communicate with the market have other, and perhaps higher, objectives such as promoting a special sale, or publicizing a special activity. Thus, it is necessary to distinguish the impact of promotional activity in terms of store image-building or institutional promotion and special impact promotion or sales-related promotion.

Consider, for instance, a retail store that is catering to middle class consumers in a beach community located in the Southeast. The store appeals to the residents of a middle to lower-middle class beach community. The store does reasonably well with its special sales that are advertised in the local paper and with discount coupons. However, studies have shown that the customers don't go there because they like the atmosphere, ambience, people,or the like. They go there because of the sales. Hence, there is not much store loyalty displayed by the customers. If the management decides to cut down these special sales, the store can run into hard times. In fact, if there were management changes, which in fact happen often, and if the new management decides to cut costs by reducing special sale activity without knowing the situation well, the special sale activity subsides, and the store gets into trouble. This author has seen many such situations. For this particular store, it would be important to create better customer relations practices so that those who come to the store for special sales will also come because they like the atmosphere, the people, and other promotional practices such as in-store discounts. Thus, promotional objectives must be carefully established and must be well understood by management .

Establish Promotion Objectives

In managing the store's promotional activity (see Exhibit 10-2), the first step is identifying objectives to be achieved both in the short run and in the long run. But the short run and the long run must be balanced. If, for instance, the store wants to establish itself as a fashion leader, it cannot concentrate on selling cheap merchandise at bargain prices. Again, it is critical to reiterate that retailers are involved in promotions to communicate with their markets. But even though it may not have been intended, promotion ends up establishing, reinforcing, or modifying the store image in the long run. Thus, institutional or image-building promotions must be distinguished from sales and cash-generating promotions in the short run. Promotional objectives, as can be seen, could vary from one situation to another significantly.

Develop the Communication Mix

The second step in Exhibit 10-2 is the development of a communication mix that is most appropriate for the promotion of the store. In developing the most appropriate communication mix, the retail store must consider at least seven key areas: strategic objectives, the target audience, the size of the trading area, message components, cost considerations, the necessary lead time required, and general trade practices (Samli 1998).

Strategic Objectives: When strategic objectives are considered, we must think of two levels of strategy—the store strategy and the promotional strategy. Earlier in this book we identified different retail strategies. As those strategies are implemented and as the store image is developed, the store will identify certain promotional priorities. For instance, if the store is trying to construct an image of being a category killer, it will promote itself heavily in local newspapers and radio stations with heavy emphasis on the store variety and low prices. However, a nicher has to deal with a well-defined section of the market. This means that the store must have a very selective advertising effort by using a minority newspaper, direct mail, a specialized radio station, and a very strong emphasis on personal selling. Communicating with this special section of the market is rather difficult, but necessary for appealing to the niche and for preempting competition.

Exhibit 10-2. Retail Promotion Management

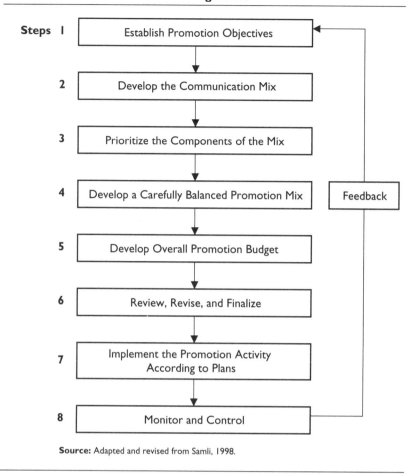

Source: Adapted and revised from Samli, 1998.

The positioner explicitly or implicitly positions itself against a specific but well-known competitor. It uses the same media as the competitor if it is competing head-on. It has to make sure that the word is out. That means, again, reaching the most people at a certain low cost. Newspaper, radio, and flyers are typical media.

The segmenter believes that consumer needs are diffused and the store has an identifiable segment (or segments) as well as a mission to satisfy that segment's needs. Communicating with a well-identified segment may call for a regional classy journal if the retail store is a rather up-scale establishment. Local TV spots may become necessary for effective competition.

The differentiator has to emphasize the characteristics of the store that are distinctive. The difference has to be emphasized through advertising, but perhaps it has to be quite visual to make a difference. More magazine and TV advertising is likely to be used to achieve the competitive edge based on differentiation.

The mass retailer has to appeal to everyone; therefore, it will try to communicate with the entire trading area at the lowest possible cost. Not the store's specific difference, but the lack thereof would be the orientation of the message. Widest reach at the lowest cost would be achieved through newspaper advertising or radio advertising.

The strategic objectives of the store must be connected to the strategic objective of the promotional activity. Strategically speaking, the promotional activity can be geared to image building, image modification, creating cash flow, or just enhancing sales volume.

Congruence between the store's overall strategy and the strategy of its promotional efforts should be positive. If the store is trying to accomplish the development of a certain image as the most comprehensive health food store in the area, but it is advertising special prices on only a few items to the public in general rather than to health food enthusiasts, there would be a major problem.

The Target Audience: It is not possible to communicate with different audiences in the same way, or reach different audiences with the same media mix. Different audiences require different types of communication. Each retail establishment has its own specific audience. It is critical for the retailer to find out what the loyal customers, for instance, need in terms of communication so that the store can effectively communicate with them.

The Size of the Trading Area: Of course, a retail establishment reaching out to a large trading area is bound to have multiple target customer groups. It will be necessary to determine if all of these target groups can be reached the same way. Alternatively, one might discern that it is possible to reach each target group differently and, perhaps, more effectively. In recent years, the borders of a trading area have become rather blurred because of cyberspace connections. Any retailer must consider the fact that there are customers outside of the trading area who are connected with the store through the Internet. The Web is a critical communication medium but it is not a distribution channel, nor is it a market all by itself. It is critical for a retailer to use cyberspace to the best advantage. This latter may change from one retailer to another.

Message Component: If the retail establishment needs to emphasize the visual as fashion merchandisers, jewelers, or some upscale furniture stores often do, then television, newspapers, glossy magazines, or elaborate brochures need to be used. If verbal communication is emphasized, then radio becomes critical. A good combination can be found on the Web. The nature of a message or the message component helps determine the overall advertising activity.

Cost Consideration: Invariably, the promotional activity is heavily dependent on the availability of funds or the extent of the promotional budget. Not all of the promotional activities carry the same price tag. Since budgets have limitations, promotional plans need to be revised to fit budgetary constraints. This particular area is discussed further later on in this chapter.

Necessary Lead Time Required: In retailing, a decision for a special sale or a promotional event may be made quickly. The promotional activity to publicize this event cannot take too much time if the timing of this event is critical. However, certain media, such as TV and magazines, may require relatively longer lead times and therefore cannot be used for that planned promotional event.

Prioritize the Mix's Components

The third step in Exhibit 10-2 is prioritization. Since there are more possibilities than what is needed, it is critical to prioritize the components of the promotion (or communication) mix. Consider, for instance, a large international antique furniture and household accessory dealer who needs to advertise regularly and often. Visual impact of advertising for this retailer is critical, since imported collectibles change and new shipments arrive often. Thus, the retailer's highest priority is to work with one of the local TV channels as an on-going activity. TV promotion for this situation is the highest priority. Brochures and print media are also high priorities.

All of the considerations discussed in the previous section come into play here. Once all the critical media are identified, then prioritization becomes the next logical step. This prioritization would include not only the mass media, but other aspects of promotional activity, such as the sales promotion, public relations, and the Internet connection. It must be reiterated that there are no formulas to optimize the promotional mix. Each retailer is responsible for that activity according to the needs and the philosophy of that particular business and its management.

Balance the Mix

Prioritization leads to balancing the promotion mix. What is going to be accomplished by the promotional activity and how it will play out in the short run versus the long run are all key considerations in developing a carefully balanced promotional mix (Exhibit 10-2).

Budget for the Mix

Unlike most of the books dealing with retailing, it is argued here that this is the point (Step 5 in Exhibit 10-2) where the promotional budget must be developed. This is a very critical consideration. Most retailing books talk about having a budget first and starting the promotion management activity afterwards. This means dollars dictate the promotional activity. On the contrary, though, the necessary promotional activity must dictate how the dollars should be used. In other words, the promotional budget is constructed by the "task objective" method. Instead of having a total sum at the outset and allocating it among the elements of a promotion mix, goals and activities of the overall communication process are first established. Then to each activity is attached a price tag. By totaling all of the price tags, one arrives at a promotion budget. This is called a *build-up* process as opposed to a *breakdown* approach.

Review, Revise, Finalize

As Exhibit 10-2 illustrates, once the budget is established by the build-up task objective method rather than the breakdown approach, it becomes vital to review and revise the promotional budget so that it will be finalized. If the task objective approach generates a budget too far from the store's ability to pay, reluctantly it will have to be reviewed and revised. Since this approach goes to the essence of what the store needs to do to implement its overall goals and its marketing strategy, the review and revision processes are difficult. Assuming the task-objective approach identifies key actions to be taken, further prioritization of the promotional mix will be required. This is difficult because originally all components of the budget were deemed essential.

Implement According to the Plan

When the budget is reduced to fit the store's financial capabilities, then the implementation of the promotional plan becomes important. If the planned promotional activity is not imple-mented effectively, then the whole undertaking becomes useless.

Monitor, Control

The implementation plans must be carefully followed, as well as monitored and controlled. Monitoring implies quick reaction to, say, commercials, coupons, or other types of promotional activity. Control implies making changes and adjustments as needed. in seeking to determine the outcome of the whole activity, attempt to generate a systematic feedback function through receiving customer opinions, looking at movements of the merchandise in the store, and measuring sales results. Such feedback activity should become routinized for the whole store performance, but it is particularly critical for the communication activity because the store's performance critically depends upon the success of communicating with one's market.

ENHANCING THE SUCCESS OF OUR COMMUNICATION

A retail establishment, any retail establishment, is constantly sending messages to consumers. Most of these messages are unplanned and uncontrolled. The way the store appears from the outside, the condition of its restrooms, all these send count-less messages. The most damaging situation in this regard is when the store believes it is sending out certain deliberate or planned messages through its efforts to promote itself and communicate with its market, but those official messages are not consistent with the informal messages that consumers are receiving. For instance, if the retail establishment, through its promotion, is maintaining that it is on the cutting edge of fashion-related devel-opments, but the store ambience is rather old-fashioned and its salespeople appear dowdy, this contradiction can be fatal.

Here, we advocate a *consistency theory*. All of the messages, both formal and informal, that are coming out of the retail estab-lishment must be consistent. Only with consistency can the retailer establish credibility, which, in turn, leads to a positive attitude towards the store on the part of its customers and encourages store loyalty.

In order to implement consistency, the retail establishment must make an attempt to control its total communication efforts with the market. Here it is of the utmost importance to bring formal and informal communication results together in such a way that the communication objectives of the store are fulfilled. Exhibit 10-3 proposes a process to enhance the promotional consistency in the store's efforts.

It is clear from the exhibit that if and when a store can determine the impact of its formal promotional efforts and compare this impact with the informal communication results, then the store can enhance its promotional consistency. Here determining the causes of informal communication that may be spreading unwanted news about the store, and eliminating them—if necessary—is required. Of course, it is not easy to find out what is being said about our store informally. However, it is possible to develop *focus groups,* or small panels which may be able to provide us with such information.

It is clear that consistency theory in retail communication means controlling our communication in such a way that negative rumors or innuendos will not derail our efforts to communicate with larger markets. By improving our sensitivity to customer

Exhibit 10-3. Enhancing Promotional Consistency

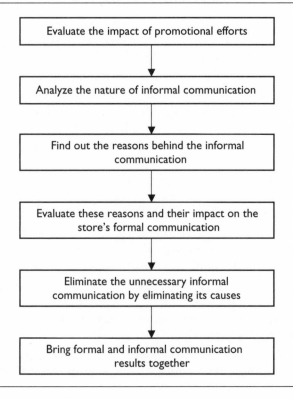

satisfaction, we can prevent negative feelings about our store. Spreading news about the store and being consistent about that news spills over to all aspects of the store. For instance, if the store is trying to project a fashion leadership role and promoting itself similarly, it cannot afford to have its salespeople looking out of style and unappealing.

SPECIAL POINTS ABOUT SMALL RETAIL COMMUNICATIONS

Perhaps above all, it is extremely improper and dangerous to say, "Well, we only have a small store and all this discussion presented here does not apply to our situation." With such an attitude, you cannot possibly survive the retail jungle. Small retailers are even more in need of positive communications with their customers.

The lack of resources because of size may be remedied by creativity. Small retailers can be very creative in their efforts to communicate with their markets and enhance their store image. Four such creative activities are articulated here. First, generating free ink, second, joint promotion, third, gift with purchases, and fourth, general ambience.

Generating Free Ink

A retailer, particularly a small retailer, can benefit greatly by generating free ink. Free ink here is public relations. The store may do something for the local poor, may support the Boy or Girl Scouts, may offer collectables, may innovate something that may be of public interest, and so on and so on. All of these and many other developments could generate a write-up in the local paper or be a news item on local TV. The value of such free ink can easily exceed the total promotional budget of the store, and it is almost totally without cost.

Joint Promotion

It is not unheard of for two retailers (or more) to promote their products or stores jointly. A local restaurant may have a fashion show by a neighboring apparel store. Similarly, a local jeweler may promote jointly with a local tourist attraction. Many stores can give promotional discounts for each other by giving discount coupons to their customers. Local museums can have a special evening with the local antique retailers. Similarly, an ice cream parlor located next to a popular restaurant may offer the restaurant's customers who do not want to eat heavy desserts some pleasing frozen yogurt combinations.

Of course, cooperative advertising is also critical here. Some manufacturers and/or wholesalers, jointly with the retailer, may promote their products in cooperative advertising efforts.

Any time we can match our target market customers with the customers of noncompeting retail establishments, we can jointly advertise or jointly offer discount credit to those who buy at our store. Such joint promotion can work synergistically to generate additional business for us and for other noncompeting retailers who are also catering to our target market. There could be many other creative promotional activities that small retailers, in particular, can use. In such cases, retailers could get together and generate fund-raisers for some charitable organization or sponsor contests that would keep our store's name before the public eye.

Gift With Purchases

Gift with purchases (GWP) is rather common in department stores, where a well-known manufacturer gives free gifts with a purchase of some specified product. In smaller retailing this would depend upon the store's orientation. Giving a red rose on Valentine's Day or giving a special gift on the customer's birthday can create much goodwill that can be considered as the store's competitive advantage. Although it may be debatable whether such gifts reflect the store's best product category, the GWP process may enhance the recognition of what is particularly good about our store and create future sales.

General Ambience

This is a special promotion category that is particularly important for the independent small and medium-sized retailer. Unlike supercenters or warehouse clubs, small and medium-sized retailers can sell genuine ambience, warmth, friendship, and casual shopping comfort. Particularly ambience here is of great importance. Not only the merchandise, displays, and the layout but also features such as music, smell, facilities (include restrooms), and the like are considered to be particularly critical in small-scale retailing. A number of studies have shown that proper selection of music and the overall aroma exuding from the store, combined with smiling faces of helpful personnel are all extremely significant in generating consumer value.

It must be restated that since this is not a textbook, actual promotional and other advertising activities are not spelled out. Advertising and retailing textbooks cover these topics very well. The key focus of our discussion in this chapter is to put forth an important philosophy of retail promotion without which advertising knowledge and mechanics have little value.

SUMMARY

In this chapter, we maintain that we, the retail establishment, must communicate with our market. In this communication process, we must promote our store image. Such promotion will enhance the name recognition of our retail establishment, it will stimulate a positive attitude in the marketplace towards us, it will change and improve our customers' attitudes, and it will even improve the attitude of the whole community towards our store.

In this chapter, we presented an eight-step promotion management plan that includes the following: establishing promotion objectives, developing the communication mix, prioritizing the components of the promotion mix, developing a carefully balanced promotion mix, developing an overall promotion budget, reviewing, revising and finalizing, implementing this promotion activity according to plans, and, finally, monitoring and controlling.

We made a distinction between institutional promotion versus cash flow–generating promotion and promotional objectives. Both are important.

Perhaps one of the most important messages of the chapter is that small retailers need promotion equally as much as their large-scale counterparts. In making the promotional activity effective, the retailer must make sure that the formal and managed messages are consistent with informal, unmanaged messages. Without such consistency, the retail store cannot be successful in communicating with its market.

Finally, four special types of promotion are advocated, particularly for small retailers. First, small retailers must learn to use free ink, or public relations, as an important promotional tool.

Second, they need to learn to be involved in joint promotional activity with other retailers. Third, seriously consider offering gift with purchases. And fourth, use ambience as a special promotion category.

REFERENCES

Samli, A. Coskun (1998), *Marketing Strategies for Success in Retailing*, Westport, CT: Quorum Books.

Developing A Merchandise Mix

In the final analysis, a retailer thrives on what it offers to its customers. Above all, a retailer offers a merchandise and/or service mix to its customers. Somehow this offering must have a value to customers so that the product or the service will be purchased. In the mind of the customer, this purchase creates consumer value and, of course, for the retailer this means survival and perhaps prosperity. The retailer has to perform a number of functions that are related to product and service assortment. This process is called merchandising. There are four key components of merchandising: *buying*, *planning*, *managing*, and *controlling*. These four components must lead to, above all, providing our customers a highly desirable merchandise mix. This mix needs to be adjusted as the needs of our target market customers change. In order to develop a desirable and adaptable merchandise mix, there must be a certain type of preplanning process, which is supported by an adjustment system. All of these considerations are preceded by an effective buying plan.

PROVIDING THE CUSTOMER WITH A HIGHLY DESIRABLE MERCHANDISE MIX

The reason for the existence of a retail establishment is to provide a desirable mix for a specific target market. The critical question here is: just what are the characteristics of a desirable merchandise or service mix? The answer will vary depending on the realities of each retail establishment. Some key considerations, however, are applicable to all retailers.

The merchandise mix, first and foremost, must be different from that of competitors. Without such a difference, the retail establishment will face an identity crisis. Not only would it not have a competitive advantage, but it also would not be able to generate a differential congruence. Although having a different merchandise mix is necessary, it is not sufficient. This different merchandise mix needs to be highly desirable to the target market of the business. It must be reiterated that if the customers are satisfied, happy, or delighted, then they become loyal to the store. There are six major retail assortment policies that a retailer can choose from.

- Deep and narrow assortments: These are typically found in specialty stores. Such stores have only so many brands and styles in their specialty areas, but they cannot have too many of each.

- Deep and wide assortments: These are appropriate for general merchandise stores. A good selection of diverse product lines that are appealing to the general public is a must. The wide selection also has depth. There are many sizes, shapes, and colors of each category. Many department stores use this approach.

- Shallow and narrow assortments: Such merchandising policies are followed by convenience stores. 7-Eleven and Lil' Champs sell only frequently needed lines with limited selection and depth at a given time.

- Shallow and wide assortments: This merchandise mix policy is most suitable for discount stores. They typically carry a large variety of generic product classes, only a few brands, and a limited supply of each.

- Consistent assortments: This is a merchandise mix philosophy that indicates the presence of consistency within departments and among departments of a retail establishment. Consistency in quality, category, selection, price,and so forth implies not having extremes of very good merchandise along with very bad. Thus, the store's merchandise and its departments are all compatible.

- Flexible assortments: The old concept of bargain basement or army surplus stores, or even second-time-around apparel shops, specifically displays such a policy. In addition to bargains and special local product lines, a flexible assortment philosophy indicates the autonomy of the local store in being able to buy locally available bargains or other unique products that may be appealing to local tastes.

CHANGING CONSUMER NEEDS AND
RETAIL MERCHANDISE MIX

Exhibit 11-1 illustrates some of the key consumer preferences that emerged during the past two decades or so. Clearly we must have a good feeling as to how these changing preferences will influence our retail store. Similarly, we must be ready to make adjustments in our merchandising policies as trends in the marketplace become noticeable. The earlier we can detect new trends, the earlier we will adjust our merchandise mix. Certainly we must have good market intelligence detecting and reporting changes and an even better feedback system that will integrate the detected changes into the store's merchandise mix.

Exhibit 11-1. Changing Consumer Needs

CONSUMER PREFERENCES	RETAILING IMPLICATIONS
Personal appearance and self-consciousness	Need for more grooming and apparel lines, along with home exercise equipment and food supplements.
To become more casual	Retailers must carry more casual products in apparel lines, lounging furniture, etc.
Better health care	Retailers must carry more exercise-related apparel, equipment, and other products, along with health foods and health food supplements.
Leisure orientation	More emphasis must be put on leisure-related products, computers, computer games, videos, DVDs, entertainment centers, etc.
Time consciousness	Retailers have to carry more efficient products, power tools, and more powerful computers and must put much emphasis on trading on the Web.
More home improvement	More retailers are providing home improvement supplies, along with advice for repair and decoration.
More pet orientation	Retailers must consider additional pet-related products and advice.

Source: Adapted and revised from Samli, 1998.

WE MUST PLAN OUR MERCHANDISE MIX

If the merchandise mix is our livelihood, we must plan it carefully. Such planning must get down to quantities, mixtures, and styles of the merchandise to be purchased and carried during certain periods of time within the constraints of a carefully prepared budget.

Earlier, in dealing with differential congruence, it was mentioned that the merchandise mix is just about the most important strategic tool to create differential congruence. Exhibit 11-2 provides a realistic perspective for merchandise mix planning in connecting it to the store's objectives. If the store has objectives to carry deep and narrow assortments because it wants to be a unique specialty store, it will have to position itself accordingly. If, say, casual wear is one of the key areas the store emphasizes but there are too few varieties, colors, and sizes, the retailer is not planning well. The other mixes of retail marketing strategy must also be adjusted. However, here our discussion is centered around the specifics of our merchandise mix. General merchandise plans typically are prepared for six-month periods and reflect the retailer's perception of the relationships and associations among various products and other variables. In the preparation of general merchandise plans, two key areas are most influential, category management characteristics and merchandise control units.

Category Management

The retail establishment that focuses on product category results, rather than concentrating on specific brands or models, would use this emerging merchandising approach. The approach arranges groupings of products into strategic business units (SBUs). Although this topic was briefly introduced in Chapter 7, it is important to take another look at it from a merchandising perspective Many retailers fail to fully understand the importance of differentiating SBUs and PCs.

In category management(CM) where entire product categories are treated as strategic business units, these categories can be customized on a store-by-store basis to generate better market performance and improve forecasting, replenishment, and overall inventory management. In large-scale retailing, suppliers are initiating a delivery-focused consumer value by taking over the whole CM. In many of these cases one supplier emerges as a "category captain" (CC) who plays a significant role in managing

Exhibit 11-2. Forecasted Merchandise Planning

KEY SELECTED PRODUCT LINES	FIVE YEARS' AVERAGE SALES (6-MONTH PERIOD)	AVERAGE INCREASE OR DECREASE* (%)	EXPECTED GROWTH IN THE LOCAL* ECONOMY (4%)	ADDITIONAL EMPHASIS (%)	FINAL NUMBERS FOR 6-MONTH PERIOD (ROUNDED FIGURES)
Suits	60,000	3.0	62,400	2.0	65,600
Shoes	10,000	7.0	10,400	3.0	11,400
Slacks	20,000	-4.0	20,800	0.0	20,000
Sports Shirts	35,000	8.0	36,400	3.0	40,200
Sweaters	8,000	-2.0	8,300	0.0	8,100
Accessories	8,000	2.0	8,300	1.0	8,500
Sports Coats	50,000	5.0	52,000	4.0	56,500

Note: Estimates are based on **8** percent growth projections in the firm's trading area. Adjustments are made on the basis of emphasis put on the line based on the firm's own experiences. Final numbers include average increase or decrease percentages. All the increases and decreases are calculated on the basis of column 1. All based on dollar control. Final numbers indicate rounding and company subjective decisions.

*For six month period.

Source: Adapted and revised from Samli, 1998.

the whole category (Desrochers, Gundlach, and Foer 2003). Although there is significant cost-saving activity, CM under the management of CC is dependent on a necessary critical volume. Since small and medium retailers do not have such a volume, they are not often engaged in CC-managed CM. On the other end of the spectrum, an outside CC cannot be as close to the store and its customers as the store management, hence in small retailing the absence of an outside CC is no great liability.

The fundamental database for category management needs to be drawn from an analysis of trading area needs. It is an important strategy of differentiation for the retail establishment in that it revolves around decisions of what to sell and what not to sell to a store's customers in its target market. In a general merchandise store, there may be a sporting goods category that is managed based on the characteristics of the target market. For instance, if the target market consists of proportionately younger people and if it is a warm beach community, the category may concentrate more on swimwear and surfing-related equipment.

Merchandise Control Units

In a more designated manner, the retail store must identify merchandise categories for which data are gathered and predictions are made. These are narrow classifications of products that are called control units. Six specific steps are identified in developing control units: deciding on control units, developing sales forecasts, planning inventories accordingly, allowing flexibility for reductions, making purchasing plans, and deciding on profit margins.

Control units are typically based on department-wide classifications such as jewelry or sporting goods. In addition to department-wide classifications, within a department classifications are also used. For instance, in the jewelry department, certain lines such as fashion jewelry, gold jewelry, diamonds, and other precious or semiprecious stones can be featured.

The utilization of control units leads to three lists that retailers must have: basic stock lists, model stock lists, and never-out lists. By using these three lists, retailers receive critical guidance as to managing the merchandise mix adequately.

Basic stock lists are detailed guidelines for key merchandise of the store with stable sales patterns. Since these patterns are predictable and their sales do not vacillate significantly, basic stock lists can be very specific and carefully detailed. Model stock lists (or stock plans) are more readily constructed for certain shopping goods and fashion merchandise. The sales of these product lines fluctuate readily; therefore, model stock plans cannot be as specific and as detailed as basic stock lists. Rather, they represent a skeleton of certain sizes, prices, quality, and color groups. Finally, almost every retailer has certain products that it is known for. The store should not be, indeed cannot be, out of these products. If a restaurant, for instance, is known for its hushpuppies, and if it is out of them every so often, this will create a credibility gap on the part of its regular customers and discourage them from frequenting the restaurant. Never-out lists represent either the core of the store's product lines, or the store is identified—at least partially—with having these products all the time. Thus, never-out lists play a critical role in the store's overall image (Samli 1998).

All three of these lists are critical in selecting control units. In small retail establishments, standard merchandise classifications may be used as control units. However, every retail establishment has its own merchandise classification as well. Commonly accepted merchandise classifications may be combined with the store's own classification. Commonly accepted merchandise classification provides various computerized information systems. Data collected this way can be modified by the store's own classification and used for merchandise mix planning. Merchandise mix plans help establish stock keeping units (SKUs), which indicate groups of merchandise arranged for inventory maintenance and control.

Sales forecasts deal with determining market potentials and their expected changes. Although many different forecasting techniques are used, we prescribe a simple general orientation. The retailer must generate three sets of information. First, changing external factors, such as personal income in the trading area or changing population in that area, must be considered. Second, internal factors, such as total sales dollars or sales units and variations in these, must be examined. Finally, the seasonality factor must be taken into account since it is particularly critical in apparel, gift items, jewelry,and similar lines. When these three variables are combined, the following formula emerges:

$$S = F(X, Y, Z)$$

Where S = Sales volume
           X = External factors
           Y = Internal factors
   and Z = Seasonal factors

If the relative role of each of these factors on store sales can be determined, then reasonable forecasts can be developed. Clearly, each store may have different experiences with these variables. Thus, the retailer must analyze its own sales and determine how these sales interact with these variables so that the sales volume can be forecast.

Exhibit 11-2 illustrates how the store's average sales have increased or decreased during the past five years. Only a few critical product lines are analyzed. It is estimated that an annual growth rate of 8 percent is applicable to the store's trading area. Calculations are based on a six-month period and half of that growth rate, namely, 4 percent, is utilized. Sales figures with expected growth are further adjusted to the store's internal changes. For instance, slacks and sweaters are adjusted downward, since they are experiencing decreasing sales. There are certain lines that the store decided to concentrate on more. The additional emphasis column in Exhibit 11-2 indicates this particular orientation. The store's management decided that sports coats, for instance, should receive further emphasis, thus a 4 percent increase is planned for this category over and beyond the expected growth in the market as well as the growth trend within the store.

Exhibit 11-2 illustrates a dollar-control orientation to merchandise planning. This whole process can easily be converted to unit control. A decision needs to be made as to which product lines should be carefully analyzed. This would depend upon the individual store.

Inventory level planning is an essential component of merchandise mix planning. The retail store cannot tie up its limited and necessary resources in an inventory that is not moving at a pace that is needed. If the store is overstocked, this can take away a large portion of its profits. It is critical that the store have adequate stocks so that it will neither lose sales nor be overstocked. As can be seen, it is essential that every retailer develop a system to plan timely purchases in adequate quantities.

It is extremely difficult to establish competitive advantage and survive in the retail jungle. With the new advances in information technology, large retailers have developed sophisticated merchandise mix planning systems. A major emerging technique for larger retailers is *collaborative planning, forecasting, and replenishment* (CPFR), by which a holistic approach to total supply chain management is accomplished. The system can deliver increased sales, organizational streamlining, and administrative and operational efficiency. As a result, cash flow improvement and return on assets advancements can materialize (Executive Summary 1999).

In order to process and fulfill orders in inventory management, quick response (QR) inventory planning and electronic data interchange (EDI) are used by large retailers quite successfully. QR enables the retailer to reduce the amount of inventory by ordering more often and in smaller quantities. EDI, on the other hand, enables the retailer to use QR inventory planning more efficiently by enhancing the computer-to-computer relationship between retailers and their vendors (Berman and Evans 2001). A retailer can use EDI to implement comprehensive strategies. EDI is a very sophisticated information network. It eliminates paperwork and facilitates fast information flow. It leads in the direction of creating more efficient ordering and receiving processes. EDI and bar-coding combined have given retailers powerful tools regarding information flow. These tools have been facilitating supplier-managed replenishment and automated ordering. Some version of *data warehousing* software dealing with managing different customer segments is also quite valuable here.

EDI and bar-coding are facilitating category management and supplier-supported merchandising, particularly in large retail establishments. They are not yet used satisfactorily by small retailers. Because of these sophisticated tools, large retailers are getting further and further ahead of small retailers. Small retailers need to find ways to use the emerging new information technology to their advantage (Samli 1998).

Planning the inventory is mainly based on three concepts: average monthly stock, average monthly sales, and planned monthly sales. The following formulas may clarify how planned inventories are constructed:

$$PI = PMS + BS$$

$$BS = AMS_1 - AMS_2, \text{ therefore}$$

$$PI = PMS + (AMS_1 - AMS_2)$$

where PI = Planned inventories
PMS = Planned monthly sales
BS = Basic stock
AMS_1 = Average monthly stock, and
AMS_2 = Average monthly sales   (Samli 1998)

145

It is essential that all retailers must be able to develop effective inventory plans. This is partly dependent on their ability to develop reasonable forecasts of monthly sales.

Planning Reductions

All retailers must understand and use markdowns. There are a number of software packages that can be used. This is more than being simply a pricing activity. But it is not strictly a merchandising activity either. Many retailers use reductions as part of their merchandising, as well as their promotional activity. But reductions also can be used for financial efficiency. Some authors consider shoplifting as part of the reduction. For whatever purpose, reductions must be built into inventory management activity.

Planning Purchases

Retailers have to plan their purchases if they want to survive in the retail jungle. It is necessary here to bring together planned sales, planned inventories, and planned reductions. Thus, planned purchases are calculated as follows:

$$PP = AMS_I + PMS + PMR$$

where PP $\quad$ = Planned purchase
$\quad\quad$ AMS_I = Average monthly stock
$\quad\quad$ PMS $\:$ = Planned monthly sales
$\quad\quad$ PMR = Planned monthly reductions

If there is a gap between planned purchases and actual purchase commitments in that much of the money is not totally committed, then there is an open-to-buy situation (OTB). This is a critical concept, particularly in small retailing, since these retailers may encounter unexpected purchase opportunities. They have to maintain some degree of flexibility by maintaining a reasonable OTB to take advantage of unexpected opportunities.

Finally, in planning purchases, it is critical to establish how much needs to be reordered. Here a concept named economic order quantity (EOQ) is used. This is the quantity in a specific number of units that would minimize the total costs of processing orders and holding inventory. Costs included in order processing are, among others, computer time, order forms, labor, and handling new products. On the other hand, holding inventory includes costs such as warehousing inventory cost, insurance, taxes, depreciation, deterioration, and pilferage. Mathematically EOQ is expressed as:

$$EOQ = \sqrt{\frac{2DS}{PC}}$$

where   EOQ   = Quantity per order (in units)
        D   = Annual demand (in units)
        S   = Cost to place an order (in dollars)
        P   = Percentage of annual carrying cost to unit cost
        C   = Unit cost of an item (in dollars)

(Berman and Evans 2002)

Such a formula can help optimize buying efforts by minimizing the costs of overstocking and the losses from understocking. The developments in information technologies (IT) are making such calculations easier. Smaller retailers, however, still have problems in developing and implementing such formulas.

MERCHANDISE MIX NEEDS TO BE CONTROLLED

Thus far our discussion relating to merchandise mix has been quantitative. However, it is important to add some serious qualitative aspects. Two special areas are emphasized here: store image versus product image, and strategic business units versus profit centers. Both of these areas provide important qualitative and managerial insights for merchandise mix control.

Store Image Versus Product Image

Although the store's product mix makes a critical contribution to overall store image, products also have their own images. For small retailers, the private brands are not particularly useful, since the market is not big enough to generate special image and resultant revenues.

Exhibit 11-3 illustrates the interaction between store image and unique products. Most small retailers may develop certain products that would attract customers. A local small bookstore is known for cookbooks. A local jeweler may be known for its diamonds. However, another local store may be carrying unusual gift items but may not have a specially known product line that is unique. As seen in Exhibit 11-3, the upper left quadrant is very

Exhibit 11-3. Interaction Between the Store Image and Its Unique Products

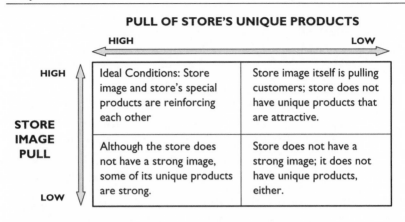

PULL OF STORE'S UNIQUE PRODUCTS

		HIGH	LOW
STORE IMAGE PULL	HIGH	Ideal Conditions: Store image and store's special products are reinforcing each other	Store image itself is pulling customers; store does not have unique products that are attractive.
	LOW	Although the store does not have a strong image, some of its unique products are strong.	Store does not have a strong image; it does not have unique products, either.

strong. A sporting goods store in a resort area may carry collector item golf clubs. If the store has a good image, its unique product line can become rather synergistic. In the lower left quadrant, these special lines may be the only feature the store has. That is rather weak. In the upper right quadrant the store may not have (more than a few) very attractive lines, but overall it has a good image. Finally, the lower right quadrant indicates the road to disaster. The store does not have enough strength to survive.

Profit Centers versus Strategic Business Units

Even a very small retail establishment is like a combination of a number of businesses in that it has various merchandise groupings. It must be understood that all of these groups do not yield the same level of profit. It would be a big mistake to eliminate some of these because they may not be yielding a desirable profit. The corner drug store in a small Southeast university town had a very active lunch counter. One day, the lunch counter was closed forever. When this author inquired as to the reasons behind this action, he was told that the lunch counter was not yielding enough profit. This author asked the store manager if he knew how much purchasing the lunch crowd had been doing after or before eating lunch. The management did not know. It is reasonable to assume that the lunch counter in this case was a strategic business unit (SBU) that brought customers to the drug store so that the store could make money from its profit centers (PCs). Not all product groups are profit centers. Some attract customers into the store so that some other more profitable products of the store are sold. Profit centers (PCs) are not adequate unless strategic business units (SBUs) can generate traffic to the store (Samli and Shaw 2002). These concepts were introduced in Chapter 7. Here they are illustrated in greater detail within the context of the retailer's merchandise mix planning and strategy.

Exhibit 11-4 illustrates the interaction between PCs and SBUs. The upper left quadrant indicates the ideal situation for a retail store or, in fact, for all businesses. Here the retail store has drawing power through its SBUs and has some appealing PCs within the store. Although, in some ways, this may be compared to good use of *loss leaders*, SBUs are way beyond loss leaders in that they generate lasting consumer value and are not just gimmicky promotional concepts. One of the keys in using SBUs is continuity. The store has certain lines that are appealing and are known to be almost always available. The lower left quadrant of the exhibit illustrates a situation where the store has profitable lines, but it is not having great success in bringing enough customers to the store. The upper right quadrant indicates that the store has strong appeal but lacks certain product lines that are profitable. Finally, the lower right quadrant illustrates an almost hopeless situation. The store is not likely to last too long because it lacks both SBUs and PCs.

Exhibit 11-4. SBUs and PCs

STORE'S PROFIT CENTERS

	STRONG	WEAK
STRONG	Strong competitive position. The store is in a most attainable success position. This is a well-managed store.	Store has strong appeals with some of its product lines, but it does not have many profitable lines.
WEAK	Store has some very profitable lines, but it is having difficulty bringing customers in	This store is not doing well; it does not have much appeal, not does it have profitable products lines. It is destined to fail.

STORE'S STRATEGIC BUSINESS UNITS

THE ROLE OF BRAND

Unlike large-scale retailers, small and medium-sized retailers cannot own or promote their own brands. Thus, the critical issue is being able to carry a brand name and related line of products that may not be available in discount stores and wholesale buying institutions. The manufacturer is, of course, interested in volume. Therefore, the manufacturer may not be interested in offering a special deal to one single retailer. However, if the small retailer can team up with other similar stores, it may be able to obtain a variation of a nationally known brand that is likely to help differentiate the retailer's store. Such competitive advantage can be very valuable. Furthermore, the small or medium-sized retailer may develop its own brands, which may be consistent or the same with the store's name. Thus, consumers know that they will find these brands only in that store.

As the retailing sector consolidates in terms of fewer large chains becoming more predominant and the mass media sector becomes more fractured because of the multitudinous mass media channels, store brands or private brands are gaining power. Procter and Gamble, Unilever, Kraft and many similar national brands that are available on retail shelves are now facing competition from, say, Kirkland Signature, which is found only in Costco stores (Boyle 2003). Although small retailers are limited in acquiring well-known upscale national brands, there have been some reasonably upscale brands that can be made available primarily to small retailers. One such brand, for instance, is "my boyfriend left me" feminine apparel line. If the brand is well known, and also known to be available only in certain stores, this can become an important asset of the retail store. There are some alternatives for a small and medium-sized retailer. It can team up and jointly carry certain brands or it can cooperate with a manufacturer initiative, among others.

BUYING THE MERCHANDISE

Unlike their large counterparts, small and medium-sized retailers do not have buyers. Managers generally cannot take time off to go to shows or visit suppliers and perform other functions that professional buyers perform. They may use a buying activity with comparable stores that are located in other cities as well as representatives from manufacturers, along with computerized buying.

Although there may be some automated buying, as discussed earlier in this chapter, much of the time owner-managers in small retailing will have to do this most essential function for survival themselves. Thus, it becomes a necessary requirement for the store manager (or an assistant) to be well prepared to buy for the store. There are at least six requirements for the manager's readiness to buy. Exhibit 11-5 illustrates these six requirements. A brief discussion of them is as follows:

If the buyer (the manager in this case) is not familiar with the trading area and does not know the people, their preferences, and behavior patterns, it will be rather impossible to purchase merchandise for the store. Familiarity with the characteristics of the trading area is essential.

The buyer for the store must also know what merchandise lines are moving and not moving. The store's SBUs and PCs must be identified and carefully incorporated into the process of buying for the store.

A good sense of merchandise quality will make it possible to have the type of quality and the level of consumer value the store is known to generate. Treating customers as members of one's immediate family, which is critical particularly in small retailing, necessitates knowing and using merchandise quality as a major strength of the store.

If the buyer for the store is not in touch with a variety of suppliers, then it will be difficult to get new merchandise or replenish the existing product lines. Thus, being in touch is essential. This type of relationship marketing is bound to be beneficial to both parties.

Perhaps one of the few advantages of small retailing is flexibility. Having a reasonably flexible open-to-buy policy enables the store to take advantage of some unexpected local opportunities.

Exhibit 11-5. The Retailer's Readiness to Buy

• Familiarity with the trading area	Understanding customers' needs and tastes
• Awareness of merchandise mix	Being familiar with merchandise availability
• Good sense of merchandise quality	Merchandise and quality knowledge
• Being in touch with suppliers	Knowing certain suppliers well
• Enough open-to-buy flexibility	Having a good control over the budget
• Good use of the Internet	Keeping in touch with suppliers

Finally, and perhaps most importantly, the retail buyer must be very interactive and comfortable with the Internet. Since the buyer is not likely to leave the store and go on shopping trips, Internet communication, along with EDI, which was discussed earlier, is a necessary tool to replace face-to-face communication effectively. Here the retailer also may establish strong relationships with foreign suppliers. Not only may there be very good bargains for the retailer to be passed on to the customers, but also many foreign suppliers are trying to enter American markets and hence they may not require certain quantity conditions that would limit the small retailer. International sourcing, therefore, can be a major source of strength for the small and medium-sized retailer.

To reiterate, the store must have an appealing and desirable merchandise mix that will provide consumer value. Buying for the store, therefore, by definition, is extremely critical to survive in the retail jungle. It is not a very common practice, but a number of small retailers may join together to buy in larger quantities and, hence, receive quantity discounts. This type of activity is likely to become more popular during the coming decades.

THE SERVICE COMPONENT

Throughout the book we have referred to the service component that retailers must keep in mind and must offer to their customers. Small and medium-sized retailers particularly must show their inclination to offer service to their customers as part of their competitive advantage. In some cases, in fact, the retailer may not have any other strength besides offering good merchandise in a pleasant atmosphere.

Certain types of retailing, such as drug stores, are much more sensitive to customers' need of services. A comparison between Walgreens and Eckerd can illustrate. By developing its freestanding stores Walgreens has been very close to populations concentrated in urban areas and has enhanced customers' needs for accessibility to a drug store. Furthermore, Walgreens has developed drive-in windows. The company has also kept longer store hours. All these services providing convenience for its customers have made the company much more profitable than its direct competitor, Eckerd.

SUMMARY

Without an adequate merchandise mix, retailers do not have much else to sell. The retailer will have to decide if the assortment will be deep and narrow, deep and wide, shallow and narrow, shallow and wide, consistent, or flexible. The retail assortment must reflect changing consumer needs.

In planning the merchandise mix, category management characteristics and merchandise control units must be identified. Identifying merchandise control units necessitates some type of forecasting, inventory level planning, planning reductions, and planning purchases. Since it is extremely critical for survival, merchandise mix must be controlled. In this control activity, decisions need to be made regarding store image versus product image and then distinguishing profit centers versus strategic business units. A new area of international sourcing via the Internet can be very beneficial. Finally, buying for a small retail store requires special skills that need to be understood.

REFERENCES

Berman, Barry, and Evans, Joel (2001), *Retail Management*, Upper Saddle River, NJ: Prentice Hall.

Boyle, Matthew (2003), "Brand Killers," *Fortune*, August, 89–100.

Desrochers, Debra M., Gundlach, Gregory T., and Foer, Albert A. (2003), "Analysis of Antitrust Challenges to Category Captain Arrangements," *Journal of Public Policy and Marketing*, Fall, 1–16.

"Executive Summary," www.cpfr.org (December 9), 1999.

Samli, A. Coskun (1998), *Strategic Marketing for Success in Retailing*, Westport, CT: Quorum Books.

Samli, A. Coskun, and Shaw, Eric (2002), "Achieving Managerial Synergism: Balancing Strategic Business Units and Profit Centers," *Journal of Market Focused Management*, 59–73.

12

Pricing is A
Powerful Tool

If a retailer wants to generate consumer value—and, indeed, a small retailer particularly cannot survive without doing so—that retailer must pay strict attention to its pricing practices. Without an adequate price, consumer value cannot be delivered. Without such delivery, there is no profit and, therefore, there is no survival. Pricing is a complex issue. Many retailers shy away from doing research and experimenting with their own pricing strategies, and hence put a lot of emphasis on the manufacturers' suggested prices. However, each retailer is different, and pricing should be, even in a small way, a part of this different identity. Although discount giants can compete exclusively on a price basis, this is not so for small and medium-sized retailers.

A critical question is whether small retailers can compete with discount giants on a price basis. After all, the discount giants get quantity discounts and take advantage of supply chain management savings, which are created by major suppliers. The small retailers, cost wise, can perform only small and less complex operations. Although important, these are not quite enough to meet discounters head on. Thus, small retailers may meet the pricing challenge but are less likely to win a price war if there is one.

The question may be asked, though: "Would consumers prefer a large place with no personality but a lot of good buys piled up, or a store with pleasant ambience, good prices, and storekeepers who like to talk to them?" The answer is not always clear cut, but the implication is that keeping our prices reasonable and competing on the basis of the uniqueness of the store and its people are more realistic approaches for small and medium-sized retailers.

PRICING OBJECTIVES

A retailer can have one of a number of pricing objectives. If making money is the first and most common objective, the retailer must understand that in the marketplace, making money is the reward that is received if and when a number of other objectives are fulfilled and consumer value is created. These other objectives can be related to sales volume, market share, rate of return to investment, positioning, or, above all, target market satisfaction (Samli 1998).

If achieving a certain sales volume is taken as an objective and if sales volume increase is desired, then the retailer, assuming a high price elasticity, may lower its prices, which would yield more than proportionate increase in sales revenues to offset the losses from reduced prices. If increasing market share is an additional objective, then other considerations will have to enter the picture also. Among these are all the other retail mixes (see Chapter 1), the store's overall appeal, its success in creating differential advantage, and the store's reputation.

Actual profit or profit expectations regarding return on investment can also play an important role in a store's pricing activity. In the short run, for instance, to create cash flow, there may be a number of *loss leaders*. Similarly, some items may be priced higher to generate greater profit in the long run. This is a proper utilization of the strategic business units (SBUs) and profit centers (PCs) dichotomy which was discussed in Chapter 7 and 11.

Target-market satisfaction must always be related to any and all of these factors and even more. If, for instance, some regular customers start complaining about certain prices, such indications must be taken into account immediately. If the target markets of the store are carefully identified and served well, the customers, as well as the store, will benefit in the long run. This is differential congruence at work, and stores' pricing decisions have a strong impact on this.

Large-scale retailers have to coordinate market share, growth, and profitability by using all of these competitive weapons, including all of their retail mixes. Here the price mix becomes very critical. In an effort to grow or to capture a larger share of the market, the large retailer may not be making enough money. In fact, it may be losing money. In other words, it may be sacrificing profit for gains in market share. Amazon.com, a multi-billion dollar retailer, did not make any money for years. Small retailers, on the other hand, are hardly concerned with growth rate or market share; therefore, they can more readily focus on their own profit picture. This can create a greater level of pricing flexibility.

PRICING GOALS

Exhibit 12-1 presents three major pricing goals, particularly applicable to small businesses. These are passive pricing, active pricing, and aggressive pricing. The exhibit also illustrates different pricing strategy alternatives in each goal.

Passive pricing implies that the retail establishment is downplaying pricing as a strategic tool. It is basically using pricing just to make the store management easier and workable. There are at least three pricing strategies that can be used to fulfill this pricing goal. Price lining is the first. This is a typical strategy to make shopping easier for customers as well as for grouping merchandise. Groups are usually specified with certain price ranges. Blind item pricing is the second strategy. By keeping a product or product line unknown and unnoticed, and pricing it slightly higher, a profit center (PC) opportunity can be created. The third passive pricing strategy alternative is copying competitors. This is simply imitating competitors in their pricing practices. This type of me-tooism can be powerful if the competitor is known for its consumer value generation.

The second pricing goal is named active pricing. Here the retailer utilizes price as a partially competitive weapon, but still the store is not known for its price discounts or the consumer values it generates. There are at least three strategies for this pricing goal. Trying to maximize the profit contribution of each and every item is proactive pricing strategy. Such direct profitability consideration calls for analyzing the contribution of each product line to the total store profit. A fixed cost plus pricing is the second strategy alternative. This simply makes pricing rather easy and practical. Every product is priced on the basis of cost plus an agreed-upon percentage such as, say, 40 percent. Cost plus a fixed margin is a common and popular approach used by many convenience stores.

Cost plus a variable margin implies more proactive pricing. Using somewhat lower mark-ups for fast-moving items and somewhat higher, but perhaps more varying, mark-ups for slower moving items can prove to be quite functional. In general, the cost plus approach is practical and popular among small retailers.

Exhibit 12-1. Pricing Goals and Practices

PRICING GOAL	PRACTICES	IMPLICATIONS
Passive Pricing	Price lining	Grouping merchandise into price categories
	Blind item pricing	Keeping a product unknown and unnoticed, and pricing it slightly higher
	Copying competitors	Pricing the way competitors are pricing
Active Pricing	Direct profitability	Trying to maximize the profit contribution of each item
	Cost plus a fixed margin for all products	Applying, for instance, 40 percent to all products
	Cost plus a variable margin	Pricing slow-moving items with higher margins and fast-moving items with lower margins
Aggressive Pricing	Leader pricing	Market leadership, aggressively lowering prices
	Skimming pricing	Charging high prices
	Pricing as a strategy	Being recognized as a low-price store
	Knock-off pricing	Slightly different merchandise but much lower prices

Source: Adapted and revised from Samli, 1998.

However, a more proactive approach to pricing may be more effective if too much dependence on cost is reduced by the attractiveness of the merchandise.

Finally, the third pricing goal is aggressive pricing. There are at least four strategies to implement this goal (Exhibit 12-1). Leader pricing means trying to establish a price leadership regarding a particular product or particular product line. In this case, the retailer aggressively lowers prices to establish a certain identity in that trading area. It may be reiterated that those products or product lines can be strategic business units for the retailer. Skimming pricing implies charging high prices and selling just small quantities. A special boutique or well-known local jeweler may be able to use this strategy selectively. A store which has a reputation for selling unique and expensive products will not succeed unless everyone knows that one receives good value there also. Some retailers may use pricing as an overall strategy. Certainly Wal-Mart does that. For smaller retailers, also, this is quite effective. The store establishes a low price image and stays with it. This could be an advantage for customers. The difficulty in this case is that the small store does not have access to the quantity discounts and low costs of large-scale logistics. Similarly they do not have the sophistication to use highly specialized information technology. Thus, the small retailer needs to be very careful in making claims of low prices if it cannot deliver. Knock-off pricing is related to carrying different merchandise and pricing it very low. If consumers know that this special line that is priced very low is available in our store, again, this can be an SBU. Making sure that products in this category are in the store's never-out lists is a critical image-building effort.

PRICING STRATEGIES VIS-À-VIS MARKET PRICES

Previous discussions regarding pricing goals and implementation strategies need to be further considered and adjusted. A retail store can develop a pricing strategy by pricing below the market, pricing at the market, and pricing above the market (Exhibit 12-2). Most retailers, in general, need to make decisions regarding the price level in the market. As the exhibit indicates, beyond the discount stores or discount department stores, small or medium-sized retailers typically cannot pursue an overall strategy of pricing below the market. The store may have a few lines as loss leaders but cannot have all of its prices below its competitors.

Most small retailers do not price higher or lower than competitors. Only prices of specific lines may change, depending on whether they are moving fast or slowly. Mostly, small retailers may differentiate themselves on the basis of other retail mixes rather than on a price mix alone.

Finally, a special jewelry store or a well-known fashionable apparel shop may price above the market. In such cases, there is "price perceived quality," which means, to a certain extent, the higher the price, the greater the perceived quality. Naturally, this means the retailer has some exclusive private brand and some of the best name brands. Some local cigar stores are also good examples. They are expected to carry expensive hand-rolled cigars rather than cheap ones.

Exhibit 12-2. Pricing at Different Market Levels

	PRICING BELOW THE MARKET	PRICING AT THE MARKET	PRICING ABOVE THE MARKET
Retail Mixes			
Product assortment	Concentration on best-selling product lines, deep and wide assortment	Deep and wide assortment	Narrow and deep assortment
Merchandise lines carried	Private labels, some name brands, special local bargains	Upscale name brands	Exclusively private brands and best name brands
Merchandise differentiation	Not differentiated, mass market appeal, exclusively price competition	Differentiated merchandise	Highly differentiated merchandise based on high image appeal
Role of fashion in assortment	Fashion follower, conservative	Concentration on accepted best sellers	Fashion leader
Service			
Personal service	Emphasis on self-service, no sales people, limited information by store personnel, no special displays	Moderate assistance by salespeople	High level assistance, extensive information, liberal returns, large variety of adjustments, etc.
Special services	Cash and carry	Some services for extra charge	Many services are included in price, such as delivery, internet connection, etc.

Store Atmospherics

Location	Poor, inconvenient site	Close to competitors	Close to customers, free-standing
Layout	Inexpensive fixtures, little or no carpeting, no paneling, limited merchandise racks	Moderate atmosphere, somewhat attractive	Very elaborate and attractive décor, many creative displays
Image	Store is known for its bargains and low prices	Store is known for its price/quality combinations, a middle class place	Store is known for its name and its quality
External Appearance			
General strategy	Modest, unassuming	Reasonably nice	Very flashy displays and show windows
Key strategy emphasis	Mass merchandiser, convenience store	Some mass merchandising, some differentiation, shopping store	Segmenter and nicher, specialty store

Source: Adapted and revised from Samli, 1998.

161

It must be reiterated that retail store pricing goals and their implementation vis-à-vis the store's price level strategies must be consistent. Inconsistency here could be detrimental to the retailer since bad news spreads fast in the marketplace.

If the store is pricing at the level that other competitors in the market are pricing, then it cannot pursue aggressive pricing goals simultaneously. The contents of Exhibits 12-1 and 12-2 complement each other and cannot go against one another.

CONNECTING GOALS AND STRATEGIES

Category killers such as Toys "R" Us or Wal-Mart, knowingly or unknowingly, use basic economic principles. If the retail prices are lowered with higher elastic demand, more units are sold. If more units are sold, then costs are being driven down. The latter can help lower prices even further and, hence, sales may further increase. Such a cost-driven pricing strategy employs aggressive pricing and keeps prices below market. Exhibit 12-2, however, makes a strong case for small retailers to keep prices at the market level. Differentiating the store rather than undercutting competition can be a less costly and more manageable strategy. Of course, it may be said once again that a neighborhood convenience store does not compete with national retailing giants on the basis of price. They exchange convenience for lower prices and they can do very well if their other retail mixes are well managed.

REMEDIAL PRICING

Over and beyond Exhibits 12-1 and 12-2, the retailer must be very concerned about, if not national, at least local economic conditions. If the local economy is very slow and the retailer's need for cash is becoming serious, the retail store may consider cutting prices almost across the board and advertising this move seriously. It is critical to realize that small retailers cannot take the position of "let us wait and see." They need to move, and they need to move fast. It must be remembered that by increasing the sales volume, it is possible to compensate for the loss of profit on each unit sold. Of course, in economic hard times, the retailer must consider revising the merchandise mix to create even more value for the price.

SPECIAL SALES AS A STRATEGIC TOOL

Argibrite's was a men's store in a university town that was owned and managed by four generations of Argibrites. The store had always done well, but twice a year it offered spectacular sales that were known and were extremely popular. The newest generation manager decided to get rid of the sales and offer slightly lower prices throughout the year. The store closed down within a year. Small retailers must understand and use special sales very carefully. This author has known of presale parties by invitation only and has often heard special sales described in words such as "the sale this year will be even better than ever before" repeated throughout the year. Even though 30 or 40 percent of the store's business may come from such events, genuine sales generate much value for the store's customers and a constant promotional activity for the store itself. Special sales can be used by any small retailer regardless of pricing goals and strategies. Planning and implementing these events are critical activities and must be taken very seriously.

SUMMARY

It is clear that without proper pricing, the retailer cannot deliver the product or the service. Pricing, therefore, is a critical aspect of retail practice if the retailer wants to survive the retail jungle. In this chapter, two key dimensions to pricing are distinguished. These are pricing goals and price levels in the marketplace. Three pricing goals are identified: passive pricing, active pricing, and aggressive pricing. A discussion of strategies implementing these goals is presented. In the case of price levels, the store can price below the market, at the market, and above the market. Perhaps one of the most important points in small retail pricing is not to have pricing goals and price levels mixed to such an extent that they contradict each other.

13

Being A Part of
A Supply Chain

In recent years, the concept of logistics has emerged as an important strategic tool. In Chapter 7 this concept was introduced as one of the five key retail mixes. It is the unique combination of these mixes belonging to our store that enables us to develop a differential congruence, which, in turn, has the potential to give us improved chances of survival and profitability. In general, logistics involves the total process of successfully moving the merchandise from manufacturer or wholesaler to our store in the most timely, effective, and efficient manner. For our small store, two phases of logistics need to be differentiated, *out-of-store* logistics and *in-store* logistics.

OUT-OF-STORE LOGISTICS

This aspect of logistics deals primarily with order processing and fulfillment, transportation, and warehousing. Out-of-store logistics in large-scale retailing has been spilling over into in-store logistics as well. By combining the two, suppliers maintain a total value delivery. In many retailing giants, therefore, these two aspects of logistics are both treated almost automatically, but in a very cost-efficient manner. This situation implies a greater decision-making role on the part of suppliers or logisticians. However, the picture is quite different in small-scale retailing. Although contacting suppliers, storing some of the merchandise outside the store, and taking delivery are all also part of small-scale retailing activities, these retailers do not have enough volume to realize the logistics savings that the giants do.

Small retailers, therefore, find themselves out of luck and not very competitive with their larger brethren. This is because small retailers cannot buy in quantities large enough to make it cost efficient for the suppliers to handle their business. Thus, small retailers are handicapped unless they can find suppliers who are more prone to using smaller volumes. Similarly, a group of small retailers may buy together. But these are not common practices. However, in contacting their suppliers, small retailers also can use EDI, bar-code, and other IT means of communication to accelerate the communication process almost as easily as large retailers. Thus, although the information flow may be reasonably good, small retailers are still handicapped, since priority is given to large volumes by the suppliers.

In large-scale retailing, many suppliers are helping to set up automated warehousing, receiving, processing, and shipping systems. In fact, these activities are being made routine by suppliers. Certainly this aspect of out-of-store logistics is not quite suitable for small retailers. Since conditions influencing the store's business may change suddenly and somewhat dramatically, small retailers would have difficulty with such routinizing activity. Small retailers need inventories replenished on a methodical routine basis, as needed. This is the key qualification—*as needed.* Because of this and because of their particular volume needs, small retailers typically cannot enjoy the savings of direct store delivery systems (DSD). Similarly, large retailers are using more and more quick response (QR) systems by which they reduce the level of inventory they usually maintain by ordering more frequently and in smaller quantities. Again, for small retailers, such QR may not be as appropriate. They may be able to order quickly because of IT procedures, but the volume requirements may be too small to receive full advantage of out-of-store logistics.

To the extent that small retailers can forecast and order electronically and meet the minimum volume requirements, they may receive some benefit from the out-of-store logistics system. Particularly some companies, such as GATX Logistics and Ryder, are beginning to help small retailers. Similarly, if some small retailers can enter into a joint agreement with some other small retailers to buy jointly, there could be more emphasis on the savings created by out-of-store logistics.

A large women's specialty retailer in Canada, for instance, has developed a distribution center. It ships millions of garments throughout 600 stores in Canada. It runs primarily on automated receiving, automated processing, and automated shipping. It has been working on its distribution accuracy, labor requirements, and processing time (Berman and Evans 2002). This is the type of out-of-store logistics that larger retailers can employ. It is still questionable whether small retailers can join with similar firms and organize a logistics system, or find other ways to create cost advantages. The small retailer must find alternate ways of cost cutting to enable them to compete with large retailers who enjoy the benefits of advanced logistics.

Although smaller and medium-sized retailers may not have the same advantages as their larger counterparts, they have other advantages. Since smaller firms may utilize a larger and more open-to-buy approach to their inventory management activity, they may buy more unusual merchandise that would appeal more readily to their target markets. These locally available lines can cut down logistics costs and make the products more readily available. This is a partial answer to the relatively less advantageous out-of-store logistics position that small retailers face.

Exhibit 13-1 presents a total picture of logistics for the small retailer. The out-of-store part of it is presented at the left hand side of the exhibit. Out-of-store logistics are based on forecasting and ordering; however, prior to forecasting and ordering, minimizing stockouts and planning the merchandise mix are critical factors that need to be handled carefully. If possible, the small retailer, just like the large retailer, would like to receive low-cost direct store deliveries (DSD). But, in the absence of DSDs, it will receive the merchandise through regular delivery.

IN-STORE LOGISTICS

In small and medium-sized retailing, in-store logistics may and should play an even more important role than out-of-store logistics. Unlike large discount stores where the merchandise is grouped and presented in a relatively unattractive manner, small retailers need to pay more attention to the physical facility. As was discussed in Chapter 9, human resources is a very critical strategic weapon for small retailers. Similarly, appearance and the overall atmosphere helps the store to differentiate itself from the competition while appealing to its customers. The overall ambience of a small retail establishment is perhaps the most critical feature that helps the store survive.

Consider, for instance, the following:

- A large retail establishment, dimly lit, with hard floors, merchandise piled in groups, and no one ever available to ask for directions or help with your choice. You are not sure where you are and where you want to go.

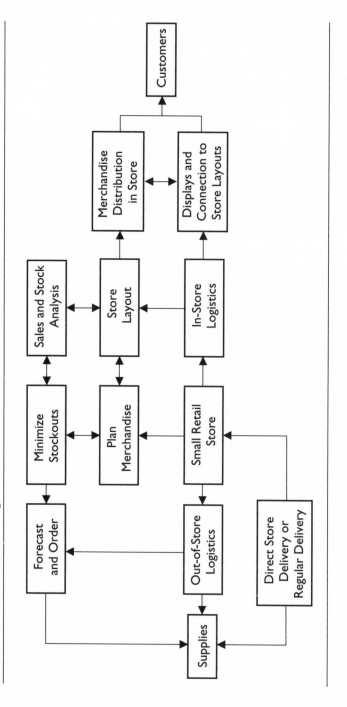

Exhibit 13-1. Small Retailer Logistics

Although some people may prefer this situation and, indeed, this particular store may have better prices, in a small retail store the atmosphere can be a great attraction. Customers feel comfortable entering a store that exudes warmth and a relaxed atmosphere, where the layout is known to them and the people are friendly. In fact, they know the people who work in the store well. Therein lies the critical role of in-store logistics.

All store have a physical layout. This particular component needs to be used properly so that merchandise distribution will be commensurate with the store's physical layout. Grouping the merchandise, displaying the merchandise in such a way that customer flow can be generated, making sure that sold merchandise is replaced and displays are not out of order, and yet providing a warm atmosphere, are all parts of in-store logistics. Whereas out-of-store logistics may be handled by dealers or distributors, in-store logistics needs to be done by the retailer. The special nuances of in-store logistics may not even be understood by dealers or distributors who are more interested in cost-cutting deliveries and cost-cutting sales.

However, if the retailer is not sensitive to the importance of in-store logistics, and issues related to it, the results can be rather severe. As indicated in Exhibit 13-1, both in-store and out-of-store logistics involve planning merchandise and minimizing stockouts.

Merchandise Planning

In Chapter 11, some of the mechanics of merchandise mix planning are discussed. In that chapter, the basic mechanics of this all-important activity are presented. It is critical to realize that small retailers particularly need to use not only the mechanics but also the art of presenting and displaying; in other words, they need to concentrate on the *esthetics* of merchandise planning.

Exhibit 13-2 illustrates some of the key parameters of merchandise planning as it relates to esthetic considerations (Progressive Grocer 1995). All retail establishments either have designers or have somebody who makes decisions regarding appearance and esthetics in conjunction with merchandise planning.

Arranging merchandise categories is not a haphazard activity. As seen in Exhibit 13-2, merchandise categories need to be arranged as if customers are doing the arranging themselves. Products must be easy to find and naturally easy to evaluate and compare.

Exhibit 13-2. The Key Elements of Merchandise Planning

* Arrange categories as customers would if they were in charge. In other words, make them easy to find, easy to evaluate, and easy to compare.

* Categories must not only be based on time, space, and product utilization, but also on how they match esthetically in terms of color, functional connection, and creating a pleasing appearance.

* Display must lead in the direction of multiple purchases by placing complementary products close to each other.

* The aim is to create unique customer value evident in the personality of the store, which value in turn adds to that personality.

* The category management reflects the needs, values, and preferences of the store's trading area.

* The retailer must as clearly know what the store should not carry as as what the store should carry.

* In managing categories, the emphasis is not only a single SKU but combining related SKUs in the form of an attractive category set.

Although it is important to categorize products in the store on the basis of *time*, say prominently displaying new models or most recent fashions, *space*, such as having fast-moving small items in one area as opposed to slow-moving big-ticket items in another area, and *product utilization*, such as displaying accessories next to most fashionable dresses, there must also be an esthetic match. Arranging the products in a pleasing manner calls for creativity, vision, and artistry. Consider, for instance, the following:

Joanny's was an upscale apparel store primarily for small, professional women. The store was located next to a Kroger store with the hopes that Joanny's would attract traffic from that store. Joanny's had good merchandise, semi-expensive accessories and jewelry. The store had an interior designer who had the background of European royalty. As such, she had a more unique vision of what the store should look like. Although, in general, it was nicely put together, the store had the appearance of European royalty. It was formal and cold. Since people from Kroger's always dressed casually just to buy groceries, they did not feel comfortable enough to enter and look around in Joanny's. The store eventually died. Interior décor and overall atmosphere were the key causes.

If the categories are carefully connected and complement each other, then, in addition to being esthetically pleasing, they may lead to multiple purchases. As opportunities for multiple purchases are planned, there may be some emphasis on joint pricing, along with an esthetic and functional matching of the merchandise. A certain evening dress may go particularly well with certain stylish accessories and, hence, such a situation may lead to multiple purchases if they are located close to each other and some discount system may be used in pricing these two groups.

Shopping in a store that is esthetically soothing, it is maintained, can psychologically create consumer value. The personality of the store, if it matches the buyer's personality, creates strong differential congruence.

Merchandise planning encompasses multiple category-management activities. Certain product category groups need to be managed in such a way that in combination they provide the perfect merchandise for the trading area of the retailing establishment in question.

It is critical for us to recognize what our store should carry. At any given time, there are numerous alternatives. We must have a strong feel for what would be appropriate and what would not in terms of the needs of our target market or our trading area.

Finally, in managing product categories, stock keeping units (SKUs) must be carefully identified, because when combined they create meaningful categories.

It is important to reiterate that retailers, regardless of size, are beginning to realize the importance of logistics. But this calls for good information about sales and a powerful insight into customer needs. Whereas this information can be obtained and, hence, distribution centers and transport capabilities can be used by suppliers, the problem is different for small retailers. Small retailers are bound by the necessity of arranging product categories and SKUs in order to provide a desirable merchandise mix to their target markets. While large retailers can use the benefits of modern logistics by allowing suppliers to manage a large part of their merchandise mixes, small retailers need to start with in-store logistics first and then decide what aspects of out-of-store logistics can become useful.

In the case of both small-scale and large-scale retailing, the entire logistics system needs to be integrated. However, small retailers must start with in-store logistics and large retailers, with out-of-store logistics.

SUMMARY

Today's retail logistics is a most powerful cost and efficiency force. In this chapter, retail logistics is divided into in-store logistics and out-of-store logistics. Modern logistics has an important contribution to make to both small-scale retailing and large-scale retailing. Certainly in both cases the retailer needs to plan the merchandise mix so that stockouts will be minimized and adequate supplies will be delivered at the lowest possible cost.

Small retailers are forced to examine sales and stock analysis to develop a proper store layout and hence pay first and foremost attention to their in-store logistics. Large retailers, on the other hand, are forced to emphasize out-of-store logistics, which are managed more by suppliers than by the retailers themselves.

REFERENCES

Berman, Barry, and Evans, Joel R. (2002), *Retail Management,* Upper Saddle River, NJ: Prentice Hall.
Progressive Grocer (1995), "Toward a Revised Theory of Category Management," August, 36.

14

Controlling the Store Performance

Retailers must have a control mechanism that evaluates overall performance and provides direction for improvement. Although it is important to evaluate the store's performance as a whole, it is also critical to evaluate some of the very specific features or activities of the store. After all, it is these specific features or activities that create a synergistic overall performance. However, behind this step by step evaluation procedure there is a learning process.

RETAILERS AS A LEARNING ORGANIZATION

Organizations, large or small, must learn continuously, since they function within markets that change continuously. However, learning takes two separate forms, proactive and reactive. A retailer, particularly a small retailer that does not have many resources to survive in the face of adversities in the marketplace, must be a proactive learner. This means that the retailer does not have much time to "just wait and see." Hence, reactive learning, even though it is taking place, is not sufficient. The small and medium-sized retailer must make a point of determining where the key decision areas in the store are and how the market responds to changes in these areas. In an earlier book (Samli 1998), this author introduced a concept called retail information management systems (RIMS). This concept must be articulated and used consistently.

Perhaps one of the most important points to be made here is that many small and medium-sized retailers would consider research as a luxury item and yet they need research-generated information even more than large retailers. Exhibit 14-1 provides a general approach to RIMS.

A learning retailer is proactive. Proactivity here implies systematic and close scrutiny of the store's activities. Every store must have what are deemed *early indicators.* There are always certain hints if some things are working or not working. For instance, the manager of a popular restaurant in a small Southeastern town is used to seeing a reasonable line of people waiting to enter the restaurant for lunch every day about 11:30 a.m. One day, as he arrives at the restaurant, he finds no one is waiting to enter. Certainly that is an indicator. The cause may be the new chef or the new menu or the new waitresses or a change in competition. What is important here, first, is the fact that the early indicator has been noticed and, second, that immediate action begin to occur to explore the reasons behind the detected early indicators. Of course, as the retailer reacts to early indicators and makes certain decisions and implements them, the subsequent reaction by the market is an important part of the learning process. As seen in Exhibit 14-1, early indicators and the market's reaction to selected decisions are inputs for control.

A retail establishment located in the downtown of a major city in the Midwest has been a specialty retailer for men's fashions. However, with the increased competition from suburban shopping centers and with some deterioration in the trading area, the store's profit picture became questionable. The reaction to early indicators of declining profit was to have a specialized line of products that would create differential congruence. It was decided that the store would carry a complete line of uniforms.

Exhibit 14-1. Retail Learning Leading to Control

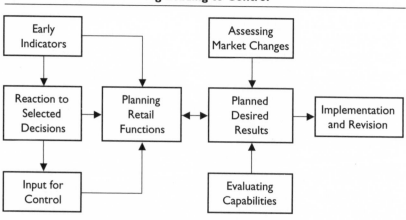

Source: Adapted and revised from Samli, 1998.

The market reacted positively, and the profit picture became substantially more desirable. The learning process led in the direction of planning the retail functions. As we learn more, these functions (such as the specifics of retail mixes) become more refined and more clearly defined. This is the value of being a learning organization and being proactive.

The past experiences of the store are crucial in regard to planning the desired results that the store aims to accomplish. Based on the specifics of the expected (or desired) results, the retail functions need to be planned. Here, understanding the changes in the market and their impact on our store is critical (Exhibit 14-1). Once the plans are implemented we go back to early indicators. If necessary, the control function takes over and further revisions to the plans take place.

RETAIL MARKETING AUDITS

Although learning and control functions are perpetual, retail establishments must make an attempt to develop formal marketing audits. There must be two such audits—internal and external.

Internal Retail Audits

Every retailer must be able to look at its practices candidly and critically. Such a look would also indicate that retailer's ability to grow. It is easy and extremely tempting to blame somebody or some force outside the store for the troubles it may have. This will help nothing. It doesn't lead to finding a solution to the problem. One small Greek restaurant in a well-off but rather old and conservative Southeastern beach community blamed the national recession for its difficulties, and as a result, the restaurant did nothing to combat negative business conditions, but simply remained a well kept secret, and went out of business. An internal marketing audit may have indicated that changes in the menu and ambience would have made the restaurant more viable.

An internal marketing audit for a retailer should revolve around at least ten key elements. Note that Exhibit 14-2 emphasizes proactive functions that enhance the retail store's competitiveness, rather than regular routine processes. In small retailing, there is a tendency to have proactive functions and regular, routine processing confused. The owner-manager may find herself being bogged down with day-to-day maintenance activity and

Exhibit 14-2. The Key Elements of A Retail Internal Audit

- Store Management's Self-Evaluation

- Store Customer Relations

- Store Personnel Management and Customer Service

- Store's Merchandise Mix and Inventory Control

- Store's Budget Controls and Spending

- Store's Ability to Buy, Its Credit and Finances

- Store's Pricing Policies and Strategy

- Store's Displays, Layout, and Ambience

- Store's Advertising and Sales Promotion

- Store's Plans for Growth

Source: Adapted and revised from Berman and Evans, 2002.

hence unable to to improve, grow, and be more proactive. Developing an internal retail audit may prevent this very serious problem of being more involved in routine activity than in making proactive plans for growth and competitiveness, and learning from the process.

Of all the ten points of emphasis, the first one is the most critical and most problematic. If the store management cannot evaluate itself and its capabilities, it will never be able to conduct an objective and constructive internal audit. After all, it is very easy to blame external forces and others for our own problems.

But performing an objective self-evaluation is a very difficult assignment. It is quite possible that small retailers, just as their larger counterparts, may need an outside consultant for such an activity. Much of the time, small retailers resist the idea of receiving help from outside consultants. However, in this case, it may be essential.

All of the other factors listed in Exhibit 14-2 have been covered in chapters throughout this book. It is difficult to prioritize these variables; some of them are more important under special circumstances. However, it is not out of line to state that displays, layout, and ambience may be considered extremely critical, particularly for small and medium-sized retailing. So are personnel management and customer service.

External Audits

Understanding the existing conditions under which the retail establishment is functioning is important for all retailers. However, it is reasonable to make a case for internal audits being even more important for small and medium-sized retailers. External audits, on the other hand, are much more critical for large retailers' performance, which may be closely tied to the existing conditions in their markets and trading areas. Additionally, large retailers are under pressure to compete with their equally large (or larger) competitors. This creates a special need for external audits examining the retailer's competitiveness vis-à-vis existing competition.

Exhibit 14-3 illustrates the key elements of an external audit. Although, in discussing internal audits, the reader is referred to the respective chapter on each item, the elements of the external audit are briefly discussed below.

The Status of the National Economy: When the national economy sneezes, the retailing sector, particularly large retailers, catches pneumonia. Some fallout may reach small retailers as well. For instance, when the economy is booming, more trendy and cutting-edge apparel may sell more readily. The Limited, for instance, did quite well during the late 1990s. Similarly, in a recessionary period, consumers may opt for classical and more durable casual clothing. During the 2000–2003 recession, Gap performed better than The Limited, and a recession is being experienced by all sectors of the economy.

The Conditions in the Store's Trading Area: A major construction activity that may divert the traffic drastically and block access to retailing facilities can be significantly critical for local retailers.

Exhibit 14-3. The Key Elements of A Retail External Audit

* The Status of the National Economy
* The Conditions of the Store's Trading Area
* Critical Changes in Immediate Competition
* Executed Changes in the Competitive Picture
* Any Unexpected Changes in the Store's Image
* New Profit Opportunities to be Pursued
* Changing Expectations of Consumers
* Emergence of New Suppliers

This author has seen a number of such cases where retailers were forced to close down their operations. Numerous changes like these may influence retailers.

Critical Changes in Immediate Competition: In much of rural America, in small towns, a phenomenon has been very noticeable during the 1980s and 1990s, the emergence of Wal-Mart. In many cases, not only Wal-Mart but a regional shopping center suddenly appears and naturally threaten the whole existing retail structure in the area. The only thing the locals can do is perhaps strengthen their regular customer relationships and join together to offer local special services and promotions. In all cases, though, the critical changes in local competition must be encountered, and some competitive measures must take place before it is too late.

Expected Changes in the Competitive Picture: If, for instance, Small Town A expects a major retailing complex to be built in Larger Town B next door, there may be many changes in the existing local competitive picture. Similarly, if, for instance, the major mall in town is bought by an outside investment company and the total profile of the mall is going to be changed and rumor has it that many imported products are to be sold there, these changes may make the local retailers think carefully and react constructively.

Any Unexpected Changes in Store Image: A small independent pizzeria in a small Southeastern university town encountered a rumor that one of its chefs had hepatitis. Without being able to resort to any kind of defense, the pizzeria went out of business. Any kind of deterioration in the store image could easily create similar situations.

New Profit Opportunities to be Pursued: When aerobics suddenly became very popular, many sporting goods stores immediately reacted by making aerobics attire and supplies available. Similarly, the emergence of frozen yogurt created many new opportunities in retailing.

Changing Expectations of Consumers: As middle class America shrank, typical middle class consumers that happened to be Sears customers changed their expectations and moved down slightly to Target and Wal-Mart. Sears responded by imitating Wal-Mart and offering "everyday low prices," but that strategy simply did not appeal to its customers, since they could go to Target or Wal-Mart for those buys anyway. Changing expectations of consumers, particularly the store's customers, can be a major shock to the retailer, particularly if that is not expected.

Emergence of New Suppliers: About three decades ago, there were not as many "competent suppliers" in the world providing a large variety of products. The so-called four tigers of Asia, i.e., Hong Kong, South Korea, Taiwan, and Singapore, all emerged during that time and became powerful participants in world trade. Now China itself has become the dominant player. American retailers, particularly small and medium-sized retailers, if at all possible, must constantly be looking for new suppliers, new product lines, and other ways of differentiating themselves from their competition. This is difficult, since small and medium-sized retailers are not quite used to international trade. This is an inevitable new activity that needs to be cultivated.

It must be noted that elements of both internal and external audits have various meanings and varying importance for different retailers. Therefore, each retailer may perhaps wish to evaluate these on a 10-point scale from "very critical" to "not very important" (Samli 1998).

OTHER CONTROL ACTIVITY

It has already been mentioned that inventory controls are critical. With modern information technology, it is possible for large and small retailers to develop a perpetual inventory control mechanism. Such mechanisms are more practical for small retailers, since large retailers have major hindrances to maintaining inventory data integrity. Such hindrances may emerge from selling errors, receiving errors, merchandise stocking errors, database errors, and physical inventory counting errors. However, as stated earlier, without a good database, inventory controls are impossible, and a store cannot possibly maintain its competitive posture. In recent years such data are used for different control calculations. Among these are gross margin return on inventory (GMROI), dollar contribution return on inventory (DCROI), and gross margin return on merchandise investment (GMROMI). Such technical analysis could provide valuable information to further set the course of the retail establishment (Samli 1998).

CONTINUOUS CONTROL ACTIVITY

Since the control mechanism leads to corrective action, and since retailing takes place in constantly changing markets, continuous control activity is a necessity.

Exhibit 14-4 illustrates the continuous control process. First, the measurement criteria need to be established. It is posited that the measurement criteria are not exclusively quantitative. They could be qualitative and attitudinal as well. As the measurement criteria describe how the store is doing, the internal and external audits provide a basis for evaluation and redirection. As discussed earlier, external and internal audits gain their value on the basis of their important criteria for the particular store. The whole activity here focuses on the redirection of the store's objectives and goals. In the meantime, the store's actual performance is evaluated and contrasted against the revised objectives and goals. The discrepancy between the two can be positive in that the store's performance exceeds the objectives and goals. Of course, the discrepancy could also be negative. In this case, feedback and further evaluation of the important store performance criteria are connected to the beginning of the total process. Obviously, the process is continuing and perhaps also changing, as indicated in Exhibit 14-4.

Exhibit 14-4. Continuous Control Process

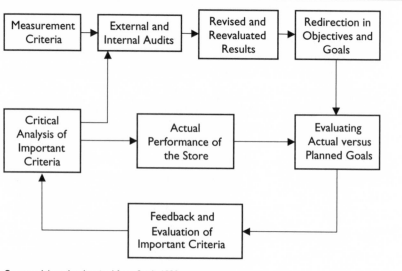

Source: Adapted and revised from Samli, 1998.

SUMMARY

This chapter, at the outset, posits that the retail establishment must be a learning organization so that it can improve its plans and its performance. Systematic audits are necessary for both learning and control purposes. Two types of audits are identified here, internal and external. These audits provide the foundation for evaluating the store's performance and direction for its goals and objectives.

Finally, it is maintained that the control process must be continuous. Since retailing is a very dynamic undertaking occurring in an ever-changing market system, the continuity of the control function can provide corrective action and improvement in retail activities.

REFERENCES

Berman, Barry, and Evans, Joel R. (2001), *Retail Management,* Upper Saddle River, NJ: Prentice Hall.

Samli, A. Coskun (1998), *Strategic Marketing for Success in Retailing,* Westport, CT: Quorum Books.

Postscript

A brief postscript is in order here to pull the whole set of ideas and experiences together and highlight the key points of this book.

- First, small and medium-sized entrepreneurial retailers are here to stay; however, they need to become more sensitive to what they are exactly and what they should do.

- Second, and perhaps most important, whereas large-scale retailers are very sensitive to national economic trends and must carefully analyze what their competitors are doing, medium-sized and small retailers are more concerned about local trends and consumer sentiments. They are geared more toward catering to their well-defined target markets or niches than worrying what the national trends are.

- Third, as national retail giants try to offer more standardized products and services at a reasonable cost, medium-sized and small retailers concentrate on more localized and specialized merchandise. In fact, this is one major way they distinguish themselves from retailing giants.

- Fourth, medium-sized and small retailers provide more personalized services. In one sense they truly benefit from relationship marketing, which is aimed at long-term mutual understanding with their regular customers.

- Fifth, while most cost-driven national retail giants offer a physical atmosphere of no distinction, small and medium-sized retailers ought to always offer a more attractive ambience so as to make their customers comfortable and at ease.

- Sixth, national retailing giants have a tendency of computerizing and hence somewhat dehumanizing retailing, whereas medium-sized and small retailers thrive on the "humanness" of their customers and their appreciation of that.

- Seventh, as a result of item six above, small and medium-sized retailers must become more genuine *learning* organizations, as their gigantic national brethren pursue automating ordering, warehousing, and logistics activities. They must learn what works and what does not work at the local level and must always be in tune with the sentiments of their customers.

- Eight, it is the medium-sized and small retailers who create jobs and generate innovations that will make the local economies and their target market customers happy. Local political authorities must be very cognizant of this aspect of entrepreneurial retailing.

- Ninth, owner-managers of small and medium-sized retailer establishments deal not only with economic and managerial issues but also with psychological issues pertaining to their customers. Hence, they have to be multi-talented in order to generate consumer value for their customers. They must also have personnel with the same skills and talents.

- Tenth, owner-managers of medium-sized and small retailer stores must understand that there is a clear-cut tie between theory and practice. The more they can bring the two together, the greater their probabilities of success. There are no limits to entrepreneurship that generates consumer value and creates differential congruence.

Throughout this book we tried to distinguish between the problems and practices of national retailing giants and the entrepreneurial behavior of small and medium-sized retailers. Our target of communication has primarily been these latter two groups. As the national population further disperses and new neighborhoods emerge, the opportunities for such retailers will be greater.

This book is primarily written for them. They must be proactive enough to take advantage of these opportunities. All in all, they must understand the importance of their being *extremely* sensitive to local needs and realizing that this sensitivity heightens their prospects for success.

It is certainly hoped that economic, social, and political conditions influencing the prospects for medium-sized and small retailers will become more favorable in time so that they can do the job of generating consumer value in our complex and challenging market system.

In discussing management of the retail establishment, time and again, the differential congruence principle has been discussed throughout this book. The retail establishment can do well by differentiating itself on the basis of target market preferences. Such congruence creates store loyalty, which is absolutely critical for the retailer. Because they are more versatile and flexible than their gigantic counterparts, small and medium-sized retailers can be more successful in achieving differential congruence, which, in essence, indicates the presence of strong competitive advantage.

Finally, implied throughout the book but not articulated is the position that market research is not only for larger retailers but for all retailers. The new generation of entrepreneurial and successful retail managers will have to be knowledgeable and proactive in planning and using research findings for their decision processes.

One last word about this book can be spoken. This was not meant to be a "how-to" book. Instead of step-by-step recipes, entrepreneurship is emphasized. Throughout the pages of this publication, reasoning, decision making, bringing theory and practice together, and strategic thinking have been emphasized. It is certainly hoped that these goals, central to this book, will pay off in the successes of its readers: young, modern, and ambitious retailing entrepreneurs who are successful in creating consumer value and running a profitable business.

INDEX

A BRIEF RÉSUMÉ

A. Coskun Samli (September 2003)

Dr. A. Coskun (Josh) Samli is Research Professor of Marketing and International Business at the University of North Florida. Dr. Samli received his bachelor's degree from Istanbul Academy of Commercial Sciences, his MBA is from the University of Detroit, and his Ph.D. is from Michigan State University. As a Ford Foundation fellow, he has done postdoctoral work at UCLA, at The University of Chicago, and as an International Business Program fellow at New York University.

In 1974-75 he was Sears-AACSB Federal Faculty Fellow in the Office of Policy and Plans, U.S. Maritime Administration. In 1983, Dr. Samli was invited to New Zealand as the Erskine Distinguished Visiting Scholar to lecture and undertake research at Canterbury University. In 1985 Dr. Samli was a Fulbright Distinguished Lecturer in Turkey. He was selected as the Beta Gamma Sigma, L. J. Buchan Distinguished Professor for the academic year 1986-87. He was given a research fellowship by the Center of Science Development, South Africa, February 1995. He was awarded a fellowship by the Finnish Academy of Sciences to teach a Doctoral Seminar, June, 1999.

Dr. Samli is the author or co-author of more than two hundred and fifty scholarly articles, fifteen books, and thirty monographs. Dr. Samli has been invited, as a distinguished scholar, to deliver papers in many parts of the world by dozens of universities. He has lectured extensively in Europe, Eastern Europe, the Middle East, the Far East, Oceania, and many other parts of the world. He has been very active in the Fulbright Commission. Dr. Samli is on the review board of seven major journals. He was the first president and a research fellow of the International Society for Quality of Life Studies (ISQOLS).

Dr. Samli is a Distinguished Fellow in the Academy of Marketing Science and a past chairman of its Board of Governors. He has done some of the earlier studies on the poor, the elderly, and price discrimination. His most recent books are *Social Responsibility in Marketing* (1992) published by Quorum; *International Marketing: Planning and Practice* (1993) published by Macmillan; *Counterturbulence Marketing* (1993) published by Quorum; *International Consumer Behavior* (1995) published by Quorum; *Information Driven Marketing Decisions* (1996) published by Quorum; *Recent Developments in Marketing QOL Research* (1996), published by Quorum; *Marketing Globally* (1998), published by NTC; *Marketing Strategies for Success in Retailing* published by Quorum (1998); *Empowering the American Consumer,* Quorum (2001); *In Search of An Equitable, Sustainable Globalization;* Quorum (2002); and *Advances in Quality of Life Theory and Research,* edited Klewer 2003, and him most recent book, *Entering and Succeeding in Third World Countries,* published by Thomson Texere in 2003. His social responsibility book and his book on empowering the American consumer were both considered among the most important academic books in the United States by *Choice* magazine, which is managed by librarians.

Dr. Samli has worked with hundreds of small and medium-sized businesses as a consultant over a 40-year period. Dr. Samli has given many seminars before hundreds of business managers in Turkey, Australia, Norway, New Zealand, and other parts of the world.

Dr. Samli has had more than 20 thousand students from all over the world. Many of them are professors, successful businessmen, and statesmen. He reviews dissertations as the outside international committee member.

About The Book...

There are over a million small retailers in the
U.S. that are competing with retail giants such
as Wal-Mart and Home Depot. To survive, you
had better have a clear strategy...

As large-scale discounters and national or
international chains are handling more retail
sales volume, the very existence of small- and
medium-sized retailers is being threatened.
Online retailing has brought many more
competitors into the retail space. To even
hope to compete you must have a strategy
that establishes your business with a solid
place in the market. *Up Against the Retail
Giants* presents a strategy, not just to
survive, but also to prosper.

Dr. A. Coskun "Josh" Samli insists that the
giant retailers lack the agility to respond to
the specific demands of customers. The very
systems and processes that enable them to be
efficient keep them from responding to their
own customers. Therein lies the basis for
your success. *Up Against the Retail Giants*
shows you how to be nimble. Josh takes you
from planning your retail strategy through
managing your supply chain, pricing,
promotion, and measuring your success.

Your retail business can thrive; *Up Against
the Retail Giants* can show you how.

7751